Planes, Pranks and Pepto Bismol

Tales and Tips from a Road Warrior

by

Bob Behrent

Eloquent Books

Eloquent Books
An imprint of Strategic Book Group
P.O. Box 333
Durham CT 06422
www.StrategicBookGroup.com

ISBN: 978-1-60911-383-4

Printed in the United States of America

Book Design: Bonita S. Watson

Pepto Bismol is a registered trademark of Proctor & Gamble

Table of Contents

Introduction

Bored to tears, but patiently waiting for my delayed flight in a crowded airline gate area, I started to notice how many of the passengers were dealing with the delay. Business people were looking at their watches while nervously tapping their feet in hopes to abate the anxiety of being late for a meeting. Some were chastising the gate agent, as if they expected her to wave a magic wand and "poof," the plane would appear. Others were talking loudly on the phone trying to reschedule their meetings that were planned for today.

I noticed earlier how some people blunder through the security line, doing everything wrong, and will aggravate guys like me who are behind them, causing us to suffer further delay because they can't read a sign, follow instructions or use common sense. Then, they whine and complain that they have to catch their flight in ten minutes, when they should have gotten to the airport two hours earlier to allow for any unexpected problems.

I smiled to myself because after more than forty years of traveling for business, and quite a number of pleasure trips, I have learned how to accept and deal with travel problems and how to get around most and even prevent some. Too bad others don't understand how to do this. I see a lot of dumb things that people do. There are ways to avoid this kind of stress.

Hmm. Maybe I should get out my laptop and type something— an instruction manual, perhaps? No. No one reads instructions. Too boring, I thought.

How about just telling about all the frustrating, crazy, funny, scary and exasperating situations I have experienced—everything I have experienced and learned in all that time? And maybe I should tell it as if we were sitting in your living room sipping beer, wine or cocktails and chatting on Saturday night. That might be helpful, and more importantly, enjoyable to all business travelers and other frequent travelers. Travel veterans will relate to this as well. *Why didn't I think of that?* or, *Hey, I did that once!* they may contemplate. Perhaps this book could become the Bible for the up and coming road warriors. Well, maybe not a Bible, but certainly an entertaining and helpful guide to *our* success.

Here we go. Boot this baby up and start typing.

Chapter 1

The Dream

So you want to be in one of those glamorous careers that will take you to the magical places that you have heard about since you were a kid. You want to visit all the major cities and see the familiar buildings that you have seen on television and in the movies, like New York, Los Angeles, San Francisco, Chicago, Dallas, Houston, and other exciting places just like them. Then, onto all the foreign cities with exotic names and reputations for excitement, adventure and intrigue to complete the list.

You may want to taste the good life while in all those big, bustling cities in the United States and as many as possible elsewhere in the world. You want to make your friends envious of your travel adventures of your job's environment and you want to be the coolest guy, or gal, in town.

You may envision yourself jetting off to exotic places like London or Paris or Shanghai to conduct your business of selling or buying your high-tech, or even low-tech, widgets, gadgets or services to or from the local World Wide Whatever International, Ltd. Company. Of course, while you are sitting in a first class airline seat, receiving all the attention you deserve from one of those young, sexy flight attendants, you will be busily tapping out your Power Point presentation on your laptop computer or creating an Excel spreadsheet and looking extremely important and professional as you prepare for the big meeting.

A top notch, big shot businessperson, you are. Wow, how impressive you must look to others, because you certainly do impress yourself.

When you finally arrive at your destination, a beefy black-tie limo driver will meet you, sling all of your luggage over his back, haul it to the boot of a silver Rolls limo, then take you to your five-star hotel.

That evening you will dine at one of the finest restaurants in the big city where you have just arrived. A snooty Maître d' will seat you and a staff of waiters will attend to your every whim. Everyone will call you "Sir" or "Madam."

Later, you can imagine yourself sipping ice cold martinis at the exclusive hotel's hand-carved bar, made by German craftsmen, of fine dark oak harvested from trees deep within the Black Forest, then imported to this location for your indulgence. As the bartender caters to your every request, suddenly, the most stunning person you have ever seen, perhaps a movie star, enters the bar, walks directly toward you, sits right next to you, smiles and says, "Hello."

Yeah, sure, happens all the time.

***

Let's leave the Hollywood set and look at the reality of it all. Most likely, you're crammed in what I call a "Four-C" seat. That is a, "Crappy, Cattle-Class, Coach" seat on the way to exciting

Omaha, Nebraska. You're stuck in the middle seat with a non-stop, gabby woman in the window seat, a four-year-old kid behind you kicking your seat-back and occasionally screaming for no apparent reason, and with Gonzo, the three hundred pound weight lifter next to you on the aisle. Gonzo smells like he just finished a two-hour workout and his sweaty arms, which are up against yours, seem to confirm it. But no cause for concern, it is only a three and a half hour flight to Houston where you will change planes to one of those little cigar-shaped tin cans in which you will need to crouch down and duck-walk down the aisle to get to your seat. For now, just hope you don't get put in a holding pattern over a storm somewhere.

You are bored, so you want to get your laptop, but Gonzo is sleeping and looked really pissed-off when you made him move an hour ago because you had get up to visit the John. So you wait until he needs to get up. When he does, you quickly get your laptop from the overhead compartment, wipe your Gonzo-sweat-wet arm on his seatback and buckle back into your seat. Since the guy in front of you has his seat all the way back, you find you can't use the tray table because the computer's lid will not open all the way. So you use your computer as it is named, a *laptop*, and start to play solitaire.

Ah, yes, and then there is that sexy flight attendant, who looks more like your old aunt Gerta, only about fifty pounds heavier and thirty years older. Or worse, you could end up with the male flight attendant who looks exactly like the guy that was smiling and winking at you in the men's room just before the flight.

The breakfast amenities are superb. The gourmet favorite, Le Flakes of Corn ala skim au lait, some yogurt with a swollen foil top that squirts out on your shirt when you open it, and a golf-ball size muffin that feels as sweaty and sticky as Gonzo.

As for lunch or dinner, the snack looks like it was recovered from a dumpster in the South Bronx and tastes about the same (not that I would actually know). And what is it with this thing called *fun size* candy bars? They are about half the size of your pinky finger and there is nothing close to fun about them. You barely get a taste and it's over with. It is more like teaser candy. Lastly, I bet you can't wait until later to get that special treat—peanuts.

When you finally arrive at your destination you will wait for your bags and usually they will be close to last ones to come up. However, if you have some type of "Priority Handling" tag on them . . . they will be dead last for sure. Then you have to drag them to the car rental shuttle-bus stop or taxi stand, which is always about a mile away at the farthest end of the airport. If you are renting a car, you will usually be offered a map with your rental car. You will refuse to accept a map because you don't want to look like a wimpy neophyte, and so you get lost.

This is not a good thing if you happen to turn off the freeway exit in say, South Central, Los Angeles or somewhere near downtown Detroit, or the South Side of Chicago, you know, the proverbial "baddest part of town." Of course, you may be lucky and have someone to give you detailed directions like, "Yeah, you go down to the traffic light and keep on goin'. Then when you get to the big building on your left, you make a right and keep on goin'. Then, when you come to the cruddy area with them gang guys millin' around, keep on goin'. What ever you do, whatever happens, don't stop. Just keep on goin'."

So after a few wrong turns, one attempted car jacking and two guys honking at you and flipping you the bird, you finally reach your hotel.

Struggling with, and eventually slinging your heavy, over packed luggage out of the trunk, you notice for the first time a large gouge on the passenger side of the rental car and you know there will be a huge dispute about this when you return the car.

You will say, "It was there when I rented it!"

"I don't see any notes about it on the ticket. No sir. *You* did that."

"I did not!" And so it goes until the police are called because you have threatened to choke the guy. Then, since you will most likely be picking up the tab for the door anyway, you kick the hell out of the gouged area and relieve your tension a bit.

Once at your hotel, and after a fifteen minute wait for the guy in front of you to find his confirmation number, then his credit card, then complain about the unlucky room number he was assigned, then request a different room, it is finally your turn to check in.

Biff, the perky, spiky-haired desk clerk, checks you in, and at the same time he is smiling at you and checking you out. He finally gives you two plastic key-cards that you will discover, after hauling your bags and your tired ass to the extreme, farthest reaches of the hotel, won't work. When you get back to the desk, huffing and puffing with exhaustion, he will tell you it must be your cell phone that caused the problem. Of course, Biff the Magnificent never makes an error and he knows all about electromagnetic and radio frequency phenomenon and how your specific cell phone will erase your key cards now, but not after he reprograms them. It is strange how cell phones don't seem to erase your credit cards.

The proper reply to this is to tell Biff, along with your best Jack Nicholson, lunatic smile, is, "No. It must be the static charge from the Taser gun I carry. And if these keys don't work again, you're gonna feel the refreshing tingle of fifty-thousand volts arcing across your testicles, Biffy boy!" He will check the cards one more time before handing them to you.

In your room and unpacked you decide to get some dinner. You enter the Denny's restaurant across the street and as you stand there alone, a pimple-faced girl asks, "How many?" I usually like to say, "There're forty-five of us. I'm just the first off the bus."

Then, after a memorable meal you walk back across the street to your hotel. The meal is memorable because the flavor keeps burping up your throat and will continue to be memorable for some hours to come.

Later, you are sitting at a cheesy bar, smelling of stale beer and mold, in perhaps a dank Holiday Inn at best. You are sipping a beer and suddenly some rather rotund, bald guy with stagnant cigarette breath plops his fat ass on the stool next to you. He belches some additional sour, pungent garlic fumes, grimaces and says, "Hey, how you doin'?" Then begins to tell you what a genius he is and how successful he is in his career of selling the barbs for the making of barbed wire.

Now you are in the real world of the business traveler.

Chapter 2

The Road Warrior

"Road Warrior." That's what some people have called me. By doing battle with all the dragons of the world of business travel, jousting with customers while riding my usually trusty steed from the rental car company into the dead of night and conquering an over-abundance of traffic, then the check-in line at a hotel, I guess that classifies me as a warrior.

Mostly, I just consider myself a business person who has been blessed with the ability to sleep on airplanes and strange hotel beds, drive in any city anywhere in the world, eat three meals a day alone, put up with sacrificing my own time on weekends to get someplace for Monday or home on Saturday from an all-day Friday work day, limit the time spent with the family, and do this often. If you have, or can develop, these abilities, then you can not only tolerate, but also enjoy, this interesting career choice.

Thinking that perhaps my forty-plus years of business travel experience may have some value for the up and coming rookies, I decided to make use of my flying time and airport waiting time to type out a few thousand words to share my experiences with those who are entering, or want to enter, a career involving extensive travel.

Even the experienced traveler may learn something new. If not, surely that person will chuckle at some of the similarities of his or her own experiences and observations.

Everything included in this book relates to true experiences, but I have changed most of the names [of people] to protect the innocent [or stupid] and also to keep the some of those litigious gold diggers, which I might mention in a not-so-good light, from suing me for some stupid reason. However, I will mention real business names with opinions based upon my personal experiences. Remember, these are only *my* opinions and only really count for me. As for those that I do wind up insulting—so be it. Get a life and a thicker skin—it's a job requirement.

As for the glamour, currently, I am typing the next few paragraphs of this manuscript sitting on the floor, leaning against the wall, with my laptop plugged in behind me and recharging, at Gate Two at Bradley International Airport in Hartford, Connecticut. I've been here a few hours waiting for my delayed plane and when it's ready to go, I'm not sure I'll be able to get my stiffening body up off this floor. Surely, there is no glamour here.

If you are not a self-motivator, are thin-skinned, short-tempered, fussy, prissy, pissy, or have depression, claustrophobia, any phobia, OCD, ADD, ADHD, PMS, menopause, manopause or any other disorder that will cause you fly off the handle and beat the spit out of someone. Or if you cannot adapt to problems, situations, bad food and some occasional dirt, noise or other discomforts or annoyances, you should choose another career course.

If you cannot adapt and learn to live easily out of a suitcase while changing hotels daily, or gain the skills of packing, ironing and preparing yourself to look sharp for your customers or clients, you will not succeed for long. Did I say ironing? If you are one of those guys that think an iron is a great Christmas gift for your wife, and if you have to have her pack your clothes for you and you haven't got a clue how to take care of yourself . . . forget this career.

If you cannot let all the aggravating things that happen daily roll off your back at least eventually, and creatively deal with ever-changing situations, problems and other nuisances, you will be suicidal after one week of travel.

***

As you will learn later, in the early days of my travels I had little or no patience. It is not that I gained patience as time went on; in fact, I am now less patient as I get older. It is that one learns to accept the fact that the world is full of people who couldn't care less about you or your problems and that the abnormal is the normal of today. If you continue to let the attitudes of people to aggravate you, soon you will have an over-abundance of stress that will destroy your health. So learn to handle stress and roll it off of your back.

That is not to say you shouldn't be assertive and try to get the issues resolved without punching a hole in a wall. By all means, use my motto of "Take Control" and you will resolve things faster.

A simple method of sorting the priority of stressful situations is to ask yourself, *"Will this matter a year from now? Six months? A month? A week? Tomorrow? An hour from now?"* The more "No's" you count, the less important the incident becomes, and hence, you should write off the stress as "business as usual."

Consider that this is nothing new. For example, the troops in World War II had a good acronym called *SNAFU* for the normal, every day screw-ups in the military systems. Snafu meant: Situation Normal—All F'd Up.

Snafu still happens. Deal with it accordingly.

***

Also, I am sure you have heard of Murphy's Law. "If anything can go wrong, it will go wrong and at the worst possible time, in the worst possible way." If you take all precautions be sure it won't go wrong, it will go wrong anyway. Rest assured, when you finally *do* get the problem resolved, then very next issue will go awry as well.

There has been one saying that has stuck in my mind for a very long time: "Blessed are those who expect nothing, for they shall not be disappointed." Assuming the fact that things will most always not go exactly as you wish makes it more acceptable when they don't and more appreciated when they do go as hoped. So expect the worst and be thrilled when it doesn't happen.

Many times the things that happen are bizarre enough to convince you someone is playing a prank on you. And many times life's reality *will* play a prank on you and you had better be prepared for it.

I will share some of things I have learned to help get around these problematic situations, or at least ease the worry, which reduces some of the stress. In short, you need to become a business-traveling MacGyver. The careful reader will compile a knowledge base from this text and use it for his or her own benefit as similar situations arises. Keep in mind, this is not a schoolbook even though I occasionally make an itemized list of tips for the reader's review. Instead, this is a historical reference to some difficult and often humorous situations experienced over the years of my business travel.

***

It does not matter what your end product or service may be, or the field of technology you are in, because most all business has grown to global extents and what you have, or what you do, can usually be sold most anywhere. That is, if you're any good at what you do. If you're not, you will wash out very fast.

My personal career choice has always been in the world of electronic and electro-mechanical components. It may sound mundane to some, but to me it has been exciting and has provided a very good living. This field has been rewarding to me because of the cutting edge technologies I am able to experience, most times long before they hit the market and before the average person has even heard of the technology. Being a techie sort of guy, I am always interested in the new wiz-bang end products on the cutting edge.

The products I have sold brought me into all types of commercial manufacturing, military bases, government research facilities, and government contractors building fighter aircrafts, submarines and other high-tech military simulator devices for training and weaponry. As a preferred supplier to some of the contractors, I have been invited to launchings of nuclear submarines. I've also been able to see my equipment on Air Force One and the Presidential Command Post Plane, and saw demonstrations of brand new jet fighters. To me, that beats some barfly-good-looker saying, "Hi" any day.

It also brought me into some of largest names in technology in the commercial industrial electronics industry, which allowed me to see some incredible new technologies in their infancy, in both hardware and software stages. The consumer side of the industry, as you probably know, has evolved since the 70s to some pretty spectacular products. Think about it. Since then we came from *records*—you know, vinyl—to eight tracks, cassette tapes, Compact Disks, Beta Max, VHS, DVDs, Blue Ray, Ipods, LCD and plasma TVs, phone TVs, and we're still going. We've gone from Atari's Pong to X-Box. Wii and beyond.

Ask a teenager today about records and they may tell you about something they have accrued at the police station. Some have no idea that music once came from a pressed vinyl disk, or a clay-ceramic disk before that. And many never saw a cassette tape.

Even the entertainment world uses a myriad of electronics. I have been in the tunnels of the underground control center of Disney World, in the back rooms of Disney Imagineering, their engineering labs, and saw some of the strangest animatronics devices in their skeletal structures along with all the electro-mechanical parts and control systems to make the magic work. Also, I've been behind the scenes at Universal Studios Theme

Parks, major television network broadcast studios and many other unique places that were fascinating to see via the back room tours with an engineer.

And one never forgets seeing the real, live Cinderella eating lunch at the Disney commissary with a guy in a Goofy suit and the Goofy head on the table.

Technology in automotive electronics, now referred to as "telematics," includes GPS, radar, sonar, FLIR (Forward Looking Infrared), Bluetooth wireless devices, voice recognition systems, DVD players, some of the best sound systems available and an array of sensing, diagnostic and monitoring systems that tell the driver everything from tire pressure to when it's time for service. Drive By Wire is currently being employed in some vehicles.

Automotive future technologies are in design stages now and we have some spectacular things to look forward to. Automated traveling features are on the near horizon. One day you will get on the freeway and take a nap while your car gets you safely and efficiently to your destination and at low emissions and high economy.

Telecommunications, security devices, HD TV, computers, wireless technologies, and a whole broad spectrum of current and evolving items, have allowed me to see the forefront of the products and enabled me to track them in the evolutionary stages. Consumer GPS systems now are close to what top-secret military GPS was a few years ago.

Remember the term *car phones*? If you do, you're an older, but hopefully a more hip person, and you now call them "cell phones." (Hip? I'm not sure that word *is* hip anymore.)

***

In my early business days — and I am talking mid 1960s to early 1970s — most business travel for me was either by auto or short flights. My point of origin was northern New Jersey. So New York City, New York's Long Island, West Chester and Orange Counties, South Jersey, the Philadelphia area, Connecticut and parts of Massachusetts were all within driving distance and it was my territory. In reality I was still a kid back then and a total rookie. I started to experience things that, when in my mundane childhood, I would have never dreamed of. The realization that there are many strange things that can happen to you every day, some good and some not so good, was beginning to amaze me and I was loving it.

***

Did you ever have the feeling you were being followed? I never did. But there were times I had the feeling *I* was following someone. Hopefully, it wasn't you.

For example: The time I was on a tour through Connecticut with my boss. When we reached our first stop-hotel in Stratford, and got into the room, I flopped onto the bed only to discover the bed was like a rock. I found a plywood bed-board not under the mattress, but just underneath the bed-sheet. That had to go.

No problem, I called the front desk and had it removed. But ironically, it happened again in New London the next night, and amazingly, again in Hartford a few days later.

How many people would ask for a bed-board, and what are the odds that I followed this person and got the exact same room? I began to hum the *Twilight Zone* theme song, then looked at my boss suspiciously and thought he had arranged an elaborate prank for my benefit.

Back then, my boss was a pretty cheap guy. Maybe I should just say thrifty, or in modern PC terms, "philanthropically challenged." So, I always had to share a room with the person I traveled with, which was usually my boss. He may have been cheap, but he was a pretty good guy with a decent sense of humor. A sense of humor is a major requirement for success, especially when traveling with me. Sure he laughed every time when I hit the plywood-covered bed. After the third one in Hartford I thought he would wet his pants he laughed so hard. I got him back one morning when he answered the phone for the wake-up call. I heard the phone ring and he answered it. Back then, the voice on the other end was an actual person, usually the desk clerk or hotel operator.

When he said, "Hello," the voice said, "Good morning. This is your wake up call."

He said. "Thanks," and hung up, only to have the phone ring immediately again with, "Good morning. This is your wake up call."

"Okay!" he replied. "I'm up."

He hung up and it rang again. "Hello sir? This is your wake up call."

"I'm up, God dammit!" and he smashed the phone down.

I had my face buried in the pillow feigning sleep, but I was laughing.

It rang again. "I'm up! I'm up! Stop freaking calling me," he shouted into the phone.

"Sir, you must respond," the person said.

He began a series of expletives and unplugged the phone from the wall and I just burst out laughing. I told him I had removed the internal mouthpiece microphone from the phone's handset the night before so the clerk could not hear his responses.

He chirped an embarrassed chuckle and called me a son of a bitch, then started for the bathroom. Just then there was a knock on the door with a voice on the other side saying, "Hello? Are you awake in there? Are you all right?"

More expletives blasted the poor bastard on the other side of the door. The guy outside the door muttered something and disappeared and that ended the debacle. That trip was memorable for another reason as well.

When we arrived in Hartford and I discovered the plywood bed-board I called guest services to come and remove it. When that didn't happen by the time we got back from dinner I pulled the board out myself.

Now, what in hell to do with it? It was the size of a full-sized bed.

Ah, thank goodness for big closets.

The board was not going to fit easily into the closet. We just couldn't get it in without removing the sliding doors.

Ah, thank goodness for big closets and Swiss Army knives.

The closet had sliding doors hanging from an upper track, just like the ones I had at home. I knew a quick little trick to remove them without having to adjust them when reinstalling them simply by taking off the center guide on the floor. You could then pull the first door forward from the bottom and it would slip off the track. Then do the same with the second door.

Even with the closet opening completely unobstructed we still struggled to wiggle that board into it and jam it up against the back wall. After a few curse words and a little sweat it was in place—I think permanently. I bet it is still there today.

Finally, ready to call it a day, I discovered the TV and radio controls were in a panel on the face of the night table between the two beds. How cool was that, me being such a techie and all?

The neatest thing was the round plastic things with a dial in it. Cool, must be pillow speakers.

My boss was sitting, stretched out on the bed, talking to his wife on the phone, while I fiddled with the control, trying to get the pillow speakers to work for the TV.

I turned the switches on, cranked the volume to ten and nothing was happening. I figured maybe the wires were crossed so I took the plastic disk-like speaker from the other side and began tinkering with that one. Still nothing.

Screw it. I went down the hall to the ice machine, got a bucket of ice and bought two Cokes from the vending machine.

When I got back to the room my boss said, "Christ, it's hot in here. Or, maybe I got a fever."

"Seems okay to me," I said. "Maybe you do have a fever. Got any aspirin?"

"Yeah. In my toiletry bag," he said as be began to get up.

He paused, feeling the bed and said, "Holy shit! This bed is hot as hell."

I felt it and it was hot. Curiously, my bed felt hot also. What the hell was going on here?

Then it occurred to me—the stinking pillow speakers worked after all. Only they were hooked up to the electric blankets. How was I to know that probably some *other* technical genius prankster switched the wires and they were now the electric blanket controls?

***

Later on, while still working for the same company, I got an expansion of territory and it took me as far south as Florida and as far west as Texas. That was a big deal back then to travel "so far" for a business trip.

How times have changed. It's not unusual now to jump on a plane and fly to California, or China, or wherever in the world the job requires us to be, even if it is for just an important one-hour meeting.

Now, the world is my territory. If the business is anywhere and I need to be there to get it, just keep my airport parking space open.

We are now so spoiled with the instant communications we have at our fingertips. We have cell phones, satellite phones, pagers, PDAs, laptops, voice mail, e-mail, Blackberries, GPS, Internet and everything we need for instant information and fast gratification.

We no longer need to drive around, only to find a urine smelling phone booth, or phone booth with the ear pieces stinking of someone else's horrid cologne, that made your ear stink all day, in order to call your office to get your messages. Mister Stinky Cologne was another guy I followed for a few months on Thursdays in New Jersey.

Now, no more calling in for messages. If they need you they can find you. Or, if you need to, you can call from anywhere; no more smelly pay-phone booths.

Is it easier today? In some ways, yes, thanks to technology. But today there seems to be two main reasons why it is actually more difficult: Customer loyalty and customer service has gone the way of the dinosaur.

Most customers have developed the attitude, "Thanks for yesterday—big deal. What are you going to do for me today?" With many companies, only cost is the driving force and most customers need to have it explained to them that, "The *price* is not the cost." Some *get it* and some don't. I always tell them, service, efficiency and quality have a cost and if not provided, late deliveries or defective material can be very expensive. If the customer bleeds the profit out of the order, the seller cannot afford to do much to support the order. Additionally, this sometimes forces the sellers to cut corners and the quality always suffers. Practices like this can put a company out of business eventually.

Quality, in many cases, is discarded over price. Eventually, some companies get bitten in the backside for this practice and I love it when that happens. "I told you so," is what you want to rub in the face of the price groveling buyer, but you move on because they will just do it again and gamble that they won't have the same problems.

From the other side of the coin, you and I require the customer service from the systems we rely upon for the business traveler and you may have noticed in your everyday activities that there is little customer service out there that is worth spit. Ironically, when someone is polite and efficient, we are so shocked, pleased and surprised that we praise him or her emphatically for doing what he or she is being paid to do.

However, more and more we seem to expect more and more, but we get less and less. Maybe I'm being pessimistic but I do not see it getting better in the future. I can envision some day, a guy like me will be bitching at some I-don't-give-a-shit gate agent at NASA SHUTTLE-LINES because the Space Shuttle is delayed and he has a meeting on the moon tomorrow at 8:00 AM and the agent tells him to take a hike. Anyone willing to take bets that the food will be as bad, or worse—served out of a squeeze tube—and that many the flight attendants are the same ones I'll have on my flight today, only fatter and older?

***

One day I had an epiphany. I was thinking, *when does one graduate from "business traveler" to "road warrior?"* Is it a period of time? Months? Years? Or is it miles? Or the number of trips you take? And at what number would that be? Is it the thousandth customer you call on? Maybe in some way it is all of the above, but there has to be a more definitive graduation point.

Well, after careful thought I came up with the answer. It is when you no longer bring back those crappy airport gifts— those 'guilty for being absent' pacifiers that get you a "How nice," or "Not another T shirt," from your wife or your kid. So when there is nothing more to buy that you can't get at your local mall and when you no longer care, nor have the time or ambition to even bother to look, *that,* my friend, is when you have graduated to the status of a hardened Road Warrior.

Chapter 3

Airlines:
Memory Lane or Memory Runway

Thinking about all the airlines I used to fly earlier in my career and realizing how many have vanished I thought a little nostalgia would be in order. The recollection of these carriers also brought to mind some rather memorable experiences.

EASTERN AIRLINES

The first airplane I flew on was in 1964; I was just nineteen years old. It was an Eastern Airlines Boeing 727. What a thrill to hear the engines roar as I was pushed back in my seat by the acceleration. The hulk of metal then lifted off the ground and, "Holy shit!" I was actually flying!

When it touched down in Charlotte, North Carolina, I was off on my own to find my way in a strange new place, all thanks to Eastern Airlines.

Eastern's shuttle service was my airline of choice when traveling the Washington, DC area, or to Boston. This was in the era when jets were beginning to replace the older propeller models. The jet seemed so much quieter and vibration free as compared to the prop planes.

Prop planes reminded me of the city busses I rode when I was a kid. The smell of diesel and the vibration of the engines made me nauseous, as did the vibration of the prop planes if I happened to get a seat near the wing engines. But the old prop planes were still pretty cool at the time from the prospective of a young guy who had little experience flying.

The Lockheed L-749 Constellation was a sleek looking aircraft, looking very similar to the old WWII Lockheed P-38 Lightning military plane. First used in commercial aviation in 1947 it continued in production until 1958. It had four propeller engines and was the first airplane to have a pressurized cabin. The last ones were retired from airline use in 1967—shortly after I started to use them.

When I began to fly these *Connies*, as they were called, some of them were already twenty years old. So occasionally, while on the ground, ready to taxi out to the runway, one of the engines would backfire and burst into flames. No big deal, we were on the ground and the pilot would just shut the fuel line to that engine and it would go out. But there were always those panic mongers that were screaming and running down the aisle to the locked cabin door. I guess if I realized at the time that the fully fuel-loaded wing tanks could have blown us all to the next century, (Hey, that's now!) I may not have been so calm, but as the say, "Ignorance is bliss."

They were thrill rides when they flew through thunderstorms and it seemed that was the case for almost every flight. They would bounce, shake, rattle and drop a hundred feet in two seconds, leaving your stomach to rise and put pressure on the back of your eyeballs. You'd be swaying nauseously side to side while lightning struck around the aircraft and you thought you were going to die.

But you didn't.

That's when I discovered Dramamine.

Eastern had become the largest airline in the free world in terms of passengers boarded and was around for a long time. But eventually they made their final landing in August of 1990 on the Island of Bankrupt Airlines. Continental then absorbed them.

***

PEOPLES EXPRESS

Peoples Express was a wonderful carrier. They were for the young, tough and patient. (Hmmm, The Young, The Tough and the Patient . . . sounds like a soap opera.) They were based out of Newark, New Jersey and were around for a number of years. When Newark International Airport, now known as Newark Liberty International, closed the original and ancient North Terminal and moved all other flights to the new Terminals A and B, Peoples Express made a deal to use the dirty old North Terminal for its operations.

Peoples Express was great. No need for a reservation and like Southwest of current times, no seat assignments. It was like waiting for a bus. You would go the terminal, push and shove to get a place to wait in line, or a space on the floor, and eventually get on the flying bus.

They flew most everywhere I needed to go and they even had a frequent flyer program.

It was great for those of limited means who wanted to go on a long deserved vacation or to visit cousin Willie in Tennessee. It was also good for my cheap-ass boss paying for my cattle-class seats and sending me to Bumfart, Ohio or some other exotic destination.

It was always a hoot getting off the plane — whoops! In Plane Speak, it's "deplaning." There was no Jetway so you went down the boarding stairs usually attached to the back of a pick-up truck, trekked a distance across the tarmac through wind, rain, snow or shine, and went into the terminal. You usually would be greeted hundreds of bodies lying all over the floor—alive, of course, but just barely. These were the standbys waiting to get a seat on one of the flights. Some of those poor bastards would be camping on that disgusting yellowing tile (or was it linoleum?) floor for days. One way to pass the time was to count the blackened chewing gum spots and cigarette burns on that yellow floor.

We deplaning passengers would be dodging, weaving and stepping around and over the various lumps of humanity to get to the baggage claim. Once bags were in hand, the smelly old diesel bus would take us to the parking lot that was actually in the next town.

Once we 'debussed,' the car was only about a half-mile away. Hopefully, there hadn't a snowstorm while I was gone because my car would be buried by the parking lot plows. There were times when I forgot to put a snow shovel in the trunk and there I was, in my suit, tie and overcoat, digging with my hands and kicking snow from under the tires with my new Florsheims. Ah, the good old days.

Peoples Express bought the Denver based Frontier Airlines and expanded routes to become the fifth largest U.S. airline. They were doing so well they began construction on the new Terminal C at Newark Airport. The building grew fairly quick into a steel girder frame, then suddenly stopped and began to rust over the next few years.

It appeared that Peoples was flying in the same financial crash course as Eastern and was to be gobbled up by Texas Air, which eventually merged it into Continental Airlines.

The current Terminal C at Newark Airport was completed by Continental and they even added large additions to facilitate its current traffic at its Newark hub.

Too bad. Peoples Express was a good no frills carrier, similar to the great Southwest Airlines of today. RIP: Peoples Express - 1981 – 1987.

NEW YORK AIR

Owned by Texas Air, New York Air took over the shuttle routes from Eastern Airlines to Boston and Washington, D.C. and flew routes to thirteen Eastern states. But it was a short-lived four years and became another victim of the times and its planes also went to the Island leaving its routes to the big "C."

***

BRANIFFF

One of the best airlines in my experience was Braniff.

For a couple of years in the 70 s I spent a lot of time in the Dallas/Fort Worth region and American or Braniff had the best scheduling to, at that time, the brand new DFW Airport. Braniff was my favorite. They had such reasonable prices on first class seats I was usually able to convince Mr. Cheapskate, my boss, that it was a better deal.

The meals in first class were great. Lobster, filet mignon, champagne and occasionally some inexpensive caviar were the fare for lunch or dinner. Coach was also pretty good as well.

At that time, the *stews*, as they were once known, were hired based on their height, (so they could easily reach the overhead compartments) their weight, (so they would not be crashing into passenger's shoulders with their fat asses as they do today while stomping up and down the aisle) and their looks. (So . . . well . . . because a guy was doing the hiring.) But to be fair, today there are some skinny flight attendants that can walk the aisle without battering the aisle passengers and are tall enough to stuff an oversized bag into the overhead compartment with malice and I think I remember one from about a year ago who was not too bad looking.

One time back a number of years ago, shortly after taking off from Dallas to Newark, the 'stew' smiled at me in my first class seat and asked, "Would you like steak or lobster for dinner today?"

I chose the steak. She wrote down my request and moved to the next person.

Just then, the pilot announced over the intercom, starting with those famous two words that usually indicate a serious problem, "Well folks . . ." He continued with the explanation of how their panel indicator lights showed the forward landing gear was still in the down and locked position. They had tried several times to retract it without success.

My take on the situation was, better down and locked than up and locked. If it was up and locked the plane would certainly have to taxi under a lot more power and with a few streams of sparks from the plane's nose once it landed— what a waste of fuel that would be.

He then said the flight engineer was coming out into the passenger area to remove a floor panel so he could visually verify the gear was indeed down and locked. It was. So we were going back to Dallas for the repair.

Once we were on the ground for a while the pilot announced that we were going to be there for perhaps an hour or longer. He then instructed the flight crew to break out dinner. As the stews began their task the pilot came back over the intercom and said, "For those of you that are interested, American still has thirteen seats available on a flight to LaGuardia." With that, almost the entire plane stood up and began to empty.

You could hear the people running out the Jetway sounding like a cattle stampede. I don't mean this in a bad way, but what a bunch of morons! Thirteen seats is an unlucky number anyway.

I just sat there in amazement. There were over one hundred idiots running to fight for thirteen jinxed seats. I looked around and saw one other guy in first class looking as surprised as I was and about six people were still back in coach.

I chuckled when the stew came back over to me and asked, "So how many steaks and lobsters do you want?"

"How about one of each?" I said.

Just as the food was placed in front of me the pilot announced the flight was officially canceled. So the seven other passengers, all of the crew and I, all gathered in the first class cabin eating and drinking most of the food and wine on board and joking around and relating some travel horror stories. We were all getting a bit tipsy, except for the pilots, of course. (Clear throat here.) They don't drink. Do they?

About two hours later I waddled, fuzzyheaded, off the Braniff plane to American Airlines to get the next flight out to Newark.

When I arrived in Newark about midnight, I discovered the helicopter service I used to fly from Newark to Morristown, New Jersey, where my car was parked, was shut down for the night. But good ol' Braniff supplied a limo service to take me to Morristown.

I guess that's one of my most memorable and best cancelled flights and why I remember Braniff in a good light.

Typically, just feed a guy well; get him drunk, and the whole bad experience turns to a good thing.

Braniff eventually went to the Island of Bankrupt Airlines as well. Too bad. They were great.

***

TEXAS INTERNATIONAL

While on the subject of Texas, I wonder who remembers Texas International Airlines. I do. I used to use them to fly from Dallas to Wichita Falls, Texas.

They used an armadillo as their logo, which I thought was rather cool at the time. Being a Northeasterner I had never seen an armadillo until I went to Texas and saw a number of the armored road-kill decomposing along the Texas freeways, some stretched out and flattened and some rolled up looking like a scaled bocce ball.

I loved the good ol' boy pilot's announcement just before take off, in a slow, dragged out Texas drawl he said, "Okay y'all. We're about to head up to Whiskey Falls today. It'll take, oh, maybe thirty, forty minutes, maybe longer, maybe not. The weather is pretty nice so I bet I'll see Oklahoma from up here, but sorry you won't. But that's okay 'cause it ain't much to look at anyway.

"We'll be flyin' 'bout somewhere between the ground and twenty-five thousand feet at a speed of, oh—pretty damned fast. Gas is full, got my roadmap and flaps are draggin'. We're 'bout ready up here. So, okay girls, strap yourselves in—we're gonna try it again."

Loved it. But now Texas International is on lying alongside the road on the Island as well, right next to the armadillo.

***

TWA

I am glad that TWA is now dead and buried. I have nothing but negative thoughts about them, except maybe one. They were headquartered in Saint Louis so they were the airline of choice to travel to that city. It seemed no other airline else wanted to go there. Can't say that I blame them.

The only good experience was the time I felt like Star-Trek-Scotty beamed me to Saint Louis.

I fell asleep on the ground in Newark while in line for take-off and awoke feeling a thud as we landed in Saint Louis.

Actually, Saint Louis is not a bad city. It has its own character and it calls itself "The Gateway to the West." Its landmark Arch is an experience to visit. You can take the Klunkinator, as I call it, to the top of the Arch and it offers a pretty spectacular view. The Klunkinator is an inclinator that angles up the inside of the Arch at varying angles until it reaches the small windows at the top in the center. It clanks and whines and makes you think it is about to fall apart, but it doesn't. I'm not sure if it is the same way today or has been changed.

So why don't I like TWA? Here is my TWA story.

As mentioned, I only took TWA to Saint Louis because it was their hub and most of their flights stopped there anyway. I tried TWA to other cities and there was always a problem. One time it would be lost luggage, another time it would be a delayed or a canceled flight. Surly gate agents and nasty flight attendants added to the experience. So what's not to like?

On one whirlwind trip I flew from Newark to Los Angeles to Phoenix to Salt Lake City to Denver and then to Saint Louis, my last stop before going home, and I was forced to use TWA for the Saint Louis leg.

I arrived without a hitch. Surprise! My bag was there and I was pleased that everything was going along fine. Even the hotel shuttle was there in a minute or two after I arrived at the bus stop.

While on the shuttle I called my wife, Mary and she asked, "Where are you?"

"Saint Louis," I said.

We talked for a while then I arrived at the hotel.

The hotel, however, turned out to be the torture chamber from Hell. The shower would alternate between ice water and scalding water and neither hot or cold removed the various collections of mold colonizing in the grout lines and seams in the tile. The sink looked dirty and didn't drain very fast. The soap, when I took it out of the Saran Wrap wrapper, looked used. The plastic cups were not sealed in plastic and looked more like specimen receptacles. I cupped my hand under to faucet to rinse my mouth after brushing my teeth.

I planned to get some work done so I unpacked my laptop and papers, placed them on the desk, pulled out the wobbly chair and sat down. Suddenly, the right front leg of the desk just fell over. It reminded me of one of those old box traps with the leg just gingerly placed there to trap an unsuspecting businessman in the box. Where was the cheese?

As I retreated backward in the chair as the desk fell in my lap; my laptop, the lamp, and a pile of papers hit me, then the floor. As I struggled to catch things, including the can of Coke that dumped in my lap, the leg of wobbly son-of-a-bitch chair listed to one side and I crashed to the floor. The entire desk followed.

There I sat in the pile of rubble, desk on top of me, my pants wet with sticky Coke, pissed-off, but not seriously injured. A few expletives later I got up and began to straighten up the mess and clean myself up.

The last piece I picked up was the desk's leg. Putting it in its original place, I propped up the desk, as it was to set it up for the next victim; hopefully the manager when I reported the incident.

No more work; I was too annoyed and distracted anyway. I figured I'd get undressed, try to rinse off my pants in the bathroom and hang them to dry, and then get into bed and watch TV.

I took off my pants, and then seeing a couple walking by my window, I realized the blinds were open. I went to the window and pulled on the drapery cord.

If you already guessed that the whole damned frame collapsed to the floor, you are correct. Undaunted and unpantsed in full display of the walking couple, I considered standing on the wobbly chair to try to fix it, but thought better of it, called the front desk and demanded another room.

I wrote a letter the Ramada Inn headquarters describing the incident. *Whoops, did I give the name away here?* Shortly thereafter I received a phone call from a woman who was laughing when I answered the phone. She continued to laugh at my experience throughout the conversation. I assume because it was so bizarre. In retrospect, it was funny but certainly not at the time.

However, when she offered me two free nights at the hotel in Saint Louis, is when I began to laugh and simply said, "You've got to be shitting me!" At that point, she lost it altogether and we both laughed about it.

Screw you Ramada, Saint Louis!

All right, I got side tracked from TWA.

The next day I had a TWA flight back to Newark. When I got to the airport I called Mary, and said I was on my way home.

She asked, "Where are you again?"

"Saint Louis. See you in a few hours."

The plane boarded, but we all sat there for about two hours due to a mechanical problem, then the flight was cancelled.

I called home. "Where are you now?" she asked

"Saint Louis. The flight was cancelled and the next flight was in the morning. See you tomorrow."

Ironically, TWA got me a room at the cheapest hotel in the area: The Ramada Inn. So it was back to the Hotel Hell for the night. I was hoping for the same room so at least the unchanged sheets would have been mine.

The next morning TWA informed the Newark-bound passengers that the duct tape had not yet arrived so the plane was still broken and eventually the flight was again cancelled.

"Where in hell are you now, Bob?"

"Saint Louis, Mary. But they say we'll be out of here by three o' clock."

Three o' clock became five and five became six.

"Where are you, Newark?"

"No. Saint Louis. They just got the duct tape but they ran out of Elmer's glue so it's tomorrow morning again before this piece of shit plane is fixed. Or, so they say, and why would I doubt them?" I replied.

Hello Ramada.

Day three guaranteed the 8:00 AM flight would take off. They just didn't know what day yet. We were told that a decision would be made by 10:00 AM whether the plane would be ready to fly or not. However, at 10:30 they announced the flight was again cancelled.

"Where are you now?"

"Where the hell do you think? Saint Louis, still!"

I stomped up to the desk and demanded to see a supervisor. I didn't know about FAA rule 243 at that time but what I was demanding was applicable to the rule: to get me on the next flight on any other airline to Newark and at TWA's expense.

I was told there are no direct flights to Newark. So I told the supervisor to get me to Chicago and then connect me with any one of the dozens of United flights to Newark. They did it.

When I got to Chicago via Delta, I called Mary and asked, "So where do you think I am?

"Saint Louis," she replied

"No! Chicago! I'm making progress."

Later I discovered that TWA stood for The Worst Airline! Now I don't want to be too opinionated, but THEY SUCKED! Glad they are now on the Island.

And what happened to Rule 243? It is on the Island too. It has ceased to exist.

***

PAN AMERICAN

Pan Am or PAA and TWA were the leaders in transatlantic flights but Pan Am seemed to be the more upscale carrier across the Atlantic of the two. They always presented a glamorous image to the public. However, Pan Am had been in bad financial shape long before TWA and just could not survive. Flight 405 over Lockerby, Scotland, December 21, 1988, was destroyed by a terrorist bomb, which took the lives of 200 people, most likely pushed them further into financial ruin.

There was a brief renewal of the Pan Am name some years later but it didn't work. RIP Pan Am.

***

ALLEGHENY AIRLINES

Allegheny did a pretty good job, although they eventually went away because no one could spell their name. They flew a lot flights to the mid-west and into some southern states.

I flew them often to Ohio and Pittsburgh. Some of their planes had facing seats in the front of the aircraft. It was sort of strange sitting three across looking eye-to-eye with a fellow passenger. The oddest thing was you couldn't seem to ever get a conversation going. Once, shortly after takeoff, I smiled and said," So thanks for attending this meeting. I hope you all brought your notes."

This was followed by four blank stares and one dirty look. Very uncomfortable and very quiet the rest of the trip.

Since it was Allegheny that was the carrier for one of my early trips of fame, I will tell you about it here.

Pittsburgh was the destination for a meeting with a Westinghouse purchasing director about existing and future business. I was the sales manager and the plan was that over the next couple of days myself and one of my sales guys, John, were to be calling on the big W and other existing accounts in the area and as far as east of the Pitts to Altoona.

On this particular sunny Monday morning we headed for Newark Airport only to be halted in a serious traffic jam, caused by a multi-vehicle collision. We could see the airport but could not get to it. Needless to say, we missed the flight.

Desperate not to miss our meeting we asked about chartering a flight but it was way too much money. I still had Mr. Cheap-Ass as a boss. So the next step was to find the next flight out. Allegheny was the one that was going to get us there only about an hour and a half late. No big deal. We would rush once we got there.

As the plane approached Pittsburgh the pilot announced over the intercom, "Well folks, we're going to be in a holding pattern for a while because one runway is closed for repairs. We should have you on the ground in about thirty, forty minutes, or so."

Great. Another delay. But it turned out to be only another thirty minutes and we were finally there.

John and I retrieved our bags and got the rental car. I reluctantly asked the rental car agent for a map and was told they were out of them, but I could buy one at one of the shops in the terminal, which I did.

Since cell phones were not in existence then, I went to a pay phone, fed in some coins and dialed the Westinghouse number. The operator there put me through to the extension and it just rang for a while before being picked up by the operator again. She told me the obvious, that he was not answering, and asked to take a message.

I told her the overview of our being late, but would be there as soon as we can.

We got into the car and realized this was one hefty map. Unwrapping the map revealed it was the size of a queen-sized blanket. Folded to reduce the height I had one end in my left hand and out the driver's window and John had his end out the passenger window in order to spread it out.

Pittsburgh Airport was about twenty miles west of downtown Pittsburgh and the final destination to the Westinghouse location was about five miles beyond the city's east border. We figured it would take forty-five minutes to an hour.

An hour later we were about ten miles from the airport, stuck in another huge traffic jam caused by an overturned tractor-trailer on Highway 22. Once a single lane was cleared we began to move slowly through the area.

Ah, finally, the city of Pittsburgh, an hour and a half after leaving the airport.

Never having been to this city before, I quickly discovered that if you took a wrong turn, you would cross a bridge of one of the three rivers and it would take you several additional miles just to eventually turn around and still be lost but at the same spot where you made the wrong turn.

Finally, a total of five and a half hours late, we arrived at Westinghouse. After some difficulty finding a parking space we entered the lobby and asked to see the purchasing director.

"Oh, he's not in today," the receptionist replied.

We both stood there staring and blinking, waiting for some punch line like, "Nah, I'm just screwing with you," but it didn't come. I was speechless, only because I wanted to spew some choice verbiage not proper to business etiquette and if I opened my mouth I was afraid it would just spill out.

"In fact," she said, "He probably won't be in until Thursday."

"Is he ill?" I asked.

"No," she answered. "He went camping."

"How nice. I hope a bear eats him," I said with a smile and she looked at me quizzically.

Since there was nothing more we could do at that hour, late

in the day, we thought we should head back to downtown, find a place to have a drink, maybe an early dinner and plot a giant map course for tomorrow.

After unintentionally crossing bridges several more times and turning around we found our way to central Pittsburgh. We drove aimlessly looking for some place to stop. In the distance I could see a Hilton Hotel and figured there would be a bar or restaurant there, so pointing in that general direction I wound up going over the Monongahela River in the wrong direction again.

Finally, back in town and still not making any progress with locating a pit-stop, we rounded a corner in one of the seedier areas of the city, when John commented, "Jesus, the only thing that could happen now is that the car will break down." Ironically, a block later, it did. Not much of a surprise for a day like that.

When I turned the corner the Avis rental car choked, sputtered, bucked and finally died. I'd managed to pull over to the curb before it came to a halt, and got out to look for a pay phone. I could see at least five or six derelicts eyeing up the two guys in suits. I tried turning over the engine but there was nothing – no noise, no clicking, just silence.

I got out and opened the hood to look at the battery connection and it looked fine. As I peered over the engine looking for something obvious I realized that I had a few drunks looking with me. One slurred his words and said, "Hey. I'll fix it for you for a dollar."

Another said, "Shit, I can fix it for fifty-cents."

"Yeah, yeah," I said. "Do I hear a quarter?"

Some other guy said, "Yeah. I'll fix it for a quarter." (Pronounced *cawter)*

They stood there glassy-eyed, not knowing what to say as I closed the hood, and then said, "Sorry, guys. It's not my car. I'm calling the owner to come and get it." I headed for the movie house up the street where I was sure to find a phone booth.

Three panhandlers later I reached the urine-smelling phone booth. When I connected with the Avis office at the airport they referred me to the local office in town. I was running out of *cawters*. Finally, reaching the downtown office, the first thing the idiot asked was, "Did you try to start it again?"

Starting to boil, I wanted to rip someone or something apart and I was getting worse by the minute. I told him he better get his ass down here with another vehicle or I'm taking a bus and leaving the car here, unlocked, as a urinal for the local street people. He said some would be there but not for about a half hour.

As we waited the news spread via the panhandle's grapevine that there were two suits in a dead vehicle with no way out. We had the windows washed a several times and ran out of quarters— sorry, *cawters*—for "coffee." However, one staggering chap was nice enough to sell eleven quarters for three one-dollar bills. That sustained us until Avis arrived an hour and a half later. Needless to say, neither of us was very happy.

The Avis driver came with a tow truck so we waited as he hooked it up, all the time being supervised and instructed by the street experts. We left our luggage in the trunk of the towed vehicle and finally we climbed into the cab of the tow truck.

We eventually drove into the entrance of a parking garage somewhere in the city and ramped up to the fifth level of a garage where Avis had its mid-town rental location. It took about another forty-five minutes to complete the transfer of vehicles, paperwork and luggage, and by then it was about six-thirty in the evening of that wonderfully productive day.

With new contract tucked into the visor I began spiraling down the exit ramp to attempt again to find that Hilton. As I got to the garage exit there was an attendant shack and a barricade arm. He looked at me and in a snotty tone asked, "Where's yer ticket?"

I sort of lost it again and started yelling, "I just rented this goddamn car. I don't have any goddamn ticket!"

"Lemme see yer contract," he said, unaffected by my impatience.

I pulled the contract out of the visor and shoved it toward him. He reached into the folder and pulled out a little blue ticket and handed the contract back to me.

I snapped the paperwork from him as the barricade lifted, said nothing and screeched some rubber to the street, mumbling "asshole" under my breath.

For what seemed like a long time we drove unsuccessfully trying to avoid bridges and circumventing one-way streets until finally we were within a couple of blocks to the Hilton. Seeing a sign on one of the buildings that said PARKING I drove in, waited for the machine to spit out a ticket and drove around and up several levels until I found a space.

What originally appeared to be a short walk turned out to be a mini-marathon. The large hotel was a lot farther than it looked and when we were finally across the street from it I realized a major highway separated us from the hotel. A long barricade ran for as far as I could see and there was no way to get to the Hilton without an additional very long walk.

As we began to head back to the car I spotted a taxi. Jumping almost in front of the cab, waving my arms and shouting, he was forced to stop. "Take us to that Hilton," I ordered.

It seemed he too must have been lost because we had to go far past the Hilton, over another bridge, and then come back the opposite way to where the driver finally pulled up in front of the hotel. I paid the fare and finally we were headed for that much deserved end-of-aggravating-day cocktail. And maybe even a decent dinner.

Unbelievably, as we walked the ground floor it became apparent that the Hilton did not have a bar or a restaurant. Assuming it was on one of the upper floors I asked at the front desk where the lounge and restaurant was.

"We ain't got one right now," the clerk replied in a style not becoming a Hilton employee. He sounded like the garage attendant's brother. 'They're fixin' 'em up and they ain't done yet. Maybe come back in a week or so. They might be done then."

"You're shittin' me, ain't you?" I mimicked his style. "You mean to tell me the guests here can't get a drink or a meal here? I'd be dead in a week or so in this hotel! Where can we go for a lousy drink around here?"

He acutely sensed my growing impatience and nervously began to scratch his nose, both inside and out in an unconscious gesture. "I don't live around here, so I dunno where anything is. Sorry mister," he stammered.

I guessed "around here," to him meant *in* the Hilton. But, beginning to feel sorry for the guy I said, "Okay, pal. Sorry. It's been a lousy day for me. Can you get me a taxi?"

When the cab driver asked, "Where to?" it struck the both of us that we had no idea. I remembered I left my parking ticket in the ashtray of the rental car. We both tried to remember a street or landmark without success.

Opening the taxi's door and standing on the outside edge, as if this extra one foot of elevation was going to let me see an aerial view of Pittsburgh, I pointed to some buildings. "Over there, I think. Head over that way and we'll see what looks familiar," I stated with a confidence that was not at all there. Hey, that's a sales ability—sounding confident when you have no idea. *Yes. I am totally confident that I have no clue.*

It was only another twenty minutes later when the familiar PARKING sign appeared as we rounded a corner.

Before paying the driver I asked where there were any decent restaurants nearby, figuring he would give good advice with his tip in the balance. He named a street where there were several supposedly good restaurants and bars and proceeded to give simple directions.

The taxi drove off well compensated for his assistance. We then plodded up the winding ramps and finally located the rental car on level four.

As I was driving toward the exit of the garage I picked up the little blue ticket from the ashtray and that was when something struck me as déjà vu all over again, as Yogi would have said. So it was not the surprising that when I stopped at the same attendant shack, Mr. Cheerful said, "Now yer gonna pay. Now, gimmie yer goddamned ticket."

***

Thanks to the taxi driver we finally found a place for dinner but not after first accidentally entering a gay bar thinking it was a restaurant. Whoops! Better back out and move on. I wonder if that SOB cab driver did that on purpose? *Bastard.*

We finally ate in an Italian BYOB place and since we didn't bring our own booze we were alcohol free when we left. But this day still deserved a drink so we rode around the city streets and found a decent looking bar on the street level of some large office building.

After five o' clock Pittsburgh's working population heads over one of those damned bridges and out to the suburbs and away from the three rivers. So with mostly empty streets it was not shocking that the bar was not crowded at all.

We bellied up to the bar and ordered our well-deserved drinks. About a minute after my scotch and John's bourbon were first sipped, alongside of me appeared a chunky, fifty-ish woman with makeup packed on so thick it was cracked like a sun-baked, dry lakebed. She pushed into me, causing me to spill some of my cherished Dewar's White Label and then wobbled to the center of the barstool next to me.

She was half-drunk, wore gaudy dollar store jewelry, and had bleached blond hair with a stupid-looking red bow tied on one side. It looked like left over Christmas ribbon. She also wore a pink mini skirt with tree-trunk size thighs bulging out beneath it. A real looker. This was going to make my day.

As she stabilized onto the stool next to me she smiled with her crooked yellow teeth and asked in a slurring voice, "Hey. Yoosh guys gonna buy me a drink?"

"I don't think so lady. It looks like one more and you may hit the floor," I said trying to sound polite.

"Bullshit!" she snapped, offended. "I can drink the both of you under the table any day of the week," as if she knew what day it might be.

Plan B: ignore her. That worked just long enough for her to shout, "Billy! Another!"

She then backhanded my arm and proceeded to tell me she used to be a model, an actress, and a dancer. I'm sure she left out circus freak, sheep-shaver and hooker.

Steadfast I stared straight forward, nodding occasionally, doing my best not to show any interest but not to piss her off either. That's when she leaned back and swung her leg onto the bar. It thudded like a Virginia ham next to my drink coaster. Thankfully, my drink was in hand. It was amazing that she didn't tip the stool over backward, but then again, she might have done this before: showing her beautiful dancer's legs.

Now I was looking at this exposed chunk of flab with an intricate pattern of varicose veins that coursed like switchback roads all the way to the Grand Canyon. I didn't know whether to run, laugh or puke.

Billy, the bar tender came to the rescue and told her to sit right before she landed on her ass again. As she balanced on the stool, she dragged the ham-hock back toward the floor. He turned to us and explained she had gotten stitches in her head about a year ago doing that same trick.

Clearly pissed about the reprimand and the lack of attention from me, she moved off the stool and went to harass someone else at one of the tables near the front door. A glance to John said; let's get out of here now. Both of us downed the remainder of our libation and looked at the EXIT sign to our left. This was the way to go, not having to confront the beauty queen on the way out the front door.

With money left on the bar we quickly got up and dashed to the side door. Once through, we discovered it did not lead directly to the street. It led us into the darkened corridors of the office building in which the bar was located. But no problem, about thirty-feet away was the glass doors to the street.

Locked. The damned doors were locked!

There had to be other doors to the street so we began to traverse the dark passageways of this empty office building. This was getting creepy as our footfalls echoed redundantly inside the empty building. It began to sound like there were others following us. *Oh, no. Not the bar beauty!* Hopefully, it was a janitor, a mugger or an axe-murderer, but, oh no, not Miss Piggy-Hocks—anything but that.

Finding another door locked, we decided to bite the bullet and go back through the bar. Maybe by now she would have her yellow teeth sunk deep enough into someone else and not notice us passing through.

So there we were, back at the door to the bar. Not surprising for that day, it was also locked from the inside.

Panic started to rise when after a few minutes of pounding the non-windowed steel door no one came to open it. Spending the night in the bowels of an office building had not been a scheduled event in my adventure book yet.

A few more poundings finally brought Billy to the door. "What the hell are you two doing out here? This ain't an entrance."

"Yeah, sorry. Thought it was the men's room," I quipped to Billy.

Madam Switchback-legs was indeed settled in with some poor guy who didn't appear to mind. So when we breezed past them, she either didn't notice, or didn't remember us from so long ago.

Within a half hour we were in our hotel for the night, and aside from my key not working the first time, the rest of the night was uneventful.

***

The next morning we spread the map over the bed in my room and plotted out the day. All I can say about that day is that it turned out to be better than the first but not worth the cost of gas for the sales calls.

When we were done for the day and somewhat depressed with the results, we drove east to a motel near Altoona, which was about eighty miles from Pittsburgh proper. The customer we were planning to see the next day was currently doing a fairly large amount of business with us and we wanted to meet him for the first time and take him to a nice place for lunch.

The next morning we arrived at ten thirty and, as if a newfound magical luck befell us, Max Efram, the buyer was there—and actually waiting for us. Say halleluiah brother! It was going to be a good day.

Max looked like a high school senior from the 1950s; the blond, flattop haircut accented his short, stout, but now softening muscular frame. He wore an open collar, plaid cotton shirt that was not considered suitable business attire in those days, except for perhaps in Altoona, Pennsylvania. He spoke in a soft voice and with the demeanor of a farm boy.

We concluded a plant tour, sat down and spoke about current and future business until it was time for me to suggest, "What do you say Max, how about lunch? What's the best place in town?"

"That would be Charley's," Max answered. "Lemme git my schweater."

Yes, he said schweater, with a shush sound.

Not to break character, Max put on a varsity letter sweater with the football in the big letter "A." Back to *Happy Days.* I felt like the Fonz.

I drove for about eight or nine miles following Max's directions. I then turned left and saw what looked like a huge prison complex. "What's that Max?" I asked.

"That's the state prison. It used to be a mental institution but now it's just a prison," Max offered.

Okay, then. Nice neighborhood.

About a mile past the prison I saw we were approaching a lone clapboard, shack-like building on the left side of the road. As we got closer, my stomach began to sink when I saw the large, sloppily hand-painted sign that simply stated, "EATS." That was Charley's.

There were only ten tables and a six-seat counter inside. To say it was austere would be an understatement. The yellowing paint on the walls was adorned only by the state health inspector's grading as "Satisfactory." Worn Formica tables and steel stacking chairs appeared to have been in use since Hoover was president.

Once seated, I asked Max what was the best thing to order. He responded softly, "That'd be the steaks."

I did a double take as the waitress came to the table. She was a short, beefy woman in a stretched-tight pink waitress dress and had more facial hair than a porcupine has quills, and it was about as coarse. I'm not talking the everyday, dark Italian grandmother moustache hair – I'm talking coarse bristles that if trimmed and shaped properly, she could have passed for a werewolf.

Max just smiled sweetly at her and said, "Hiya doin' Gracie?"

Now, I know you can't judge a book by its cover but sometimes inbreeding is more than in the physical appearance. The people we were running into seemed to be from one big family. I mean one *inbred* family. I could not believe the characters we had dealt with the last two days but what happened next closed the book for me.

We had each ordered a steak. Max ordered a well done, John ordered a medium and I ordered a medium rare.

A while later Princess Grace appeared at tableside with three plates, each with a different color toothpick sticking out of the meat. "Who gits the well?"

"I do," replied Max with a big boyish smile.

"Who gits the medium?" was the next question.

"That's mine," John said.

Now, I know you are probably ahead of me here, and you are absolutely on target.

"Who gits the medium rare?" she asked without a clue.

I was speechless and thought at first she must be kidding, you know, one of those werewolf pranks. I didn't know if I should laugh or not so I just sat there for the moment.

Now she was confused because she didn't know what to do with the medium rare steak until I shook off the awe and finally said it was mine.

The steaks were just okay, about the same as Sizzler, but a little thicker. All right, they were just barely edible. Actually, they sucked. But I guess by comparison of local standards, they were the best around.

When finished, I left a twenty percent tip and the wolf-bane-beauty almost danced a little two-step thinking about the new suspenders she could buy with all that money. Maybe even a razor!

Back at Max's office, we dropped him off and said goodbye. We were then headed back to Pittsburgh Airport, about a hundred miles away. It was a somewhat long drive but judging from the trip to Altoona, we saw no problem with traffic and could clip along at fifty to sixty miles per hour without a problem. In fact, we had too much time because our flight was not until seven o' clock that evening and that was a little more than six hours away.

As we drove west John noticed a billboard advertising Indian Caverns; the exit was four miles ahead. "Hey. We have time. Want to stop and check it out?"

"Sure. Why not?" I got in the right lane for the exit.

Once off the highway at the end of the exit ramp I had no idea whether to turn right or left to get to Indian Caverns. With the odds at fifty-fifty, and the way this trip was going, I supposed it didn't matter, so I turned right.

After about five miles I was about to turn around when I saw a sign stating Indian Caverns was ahead on the left, and indeed it was.

I parked the car and went to a little ticket booth where a middle-aged woman in a frumpy housedress smiled and asked, "How many?"

"Two," I said and gave her a ten dollar bill for the five-buck admissions.

We followed a path to the cavern entrance and there we met George and Betty, a retired couple that told us they were on a national tour of caves. They were overwhelmed with excitement and enthusiasm of exploring this hole in the ground. They had already been to twelve caves in as many states and this was lucky number thirteen. Funny how that number always seems to come up.

In a short time Clem, Jed, Willie, or whatever the hell the kid's name was arrived to announce he was our sixteen-year-old tour guide. He was the ticket seller's son. I assumed this large hole was on the family's property and they were cashing in on Mother Nature's defect in the terra firma.

He had a nice smile and still had all his teeth, albeit they were green and not destined for a long term chewing epic. Some people call that *Summer Teeth*. You know, summer green, summer yellow, summer missing.

He gave each of us a cheap plastic flashlight. I was hoping for a large rubber band, or something to tie it to my head, so I could act like a hands-free spelunker. I had a strange desire to slip in with this whacky environment and make George and Betty jealous that they didn't have a headlight. But, unfortunately, I had to be an adult about it. After all, I am a professional business man.

The kid was fairly enthusiastic himself. He had all his lines and humorous script memorized. As we followed the kid, he would direct his light to some corner of a cavern and exclaim, "And there's Popeye!" and "Looky here at the two fried eggs! And over there is a freight train, better move aside."

Each time he would say something corny, old George and Betty would oooh and aaah, or laugh hysterically. It became nauseating.

I began to realize we were already in this damp hole for about an hour and still descending with the wiz-kid and the AARP explorer duo. Shining my dying flashlight on my watch, I asked how much longer the tour was going to take. The kid said not to worry because we could take all the time we wanted. It was a slow day.

Figuring the time we had left I estimated we should start back in no more than a half hour. At about the time we reached that benchmark, and since I thought I glanced a little red guy with stubby horns and a spear-pointed tail hiding behind a stalactite, I began to think we were descending way too deep for me. I told the guide we were turning around and going back, unless the tour was a loop and came out where it was shorter going ahead.

He told me we would miss the pipe organ, the best part. I told him, "I saw it in the shower this morning," then asked, "Which way do we go?"

We went back the way we came. Going back was much faster than the descent but it still took us almost forty-five minutes to reach daylight.

As we approached the rental car I saw that someone, probably one of Clem-Jed-Willie's kid brothers, had put huge bumper stickers on the car. Two were on the front and two on the back bumpers. Fortunately, they were not the sticky-back type, but they were made of heavy duty, indestructible compressed cardboard and wired on with steel bailing wire and obviously twisted tight with pliers.

There was no way in hell I was going to drive that car and turn it in to Avis with those stupid giant signs on the car. After all, as I said, we were professionals and had an appearance to keep up. Right? And besides, I never did strap the flashlight to my head.

It took us two strong, young guys almost another half hour to get those miserable "INDIAN CAVERNS" bumper stickers off and finally be on our way. We still had a reasonable amount of time.

I drove out of the parking lot, turned onto the road and headed for the highway. We got about two miles toward the highway. A short distance ahead I saw flashing red lights at a railroad crossing.

The train was slowly entering the intersection when I got there. And slow is an understatement. We sat there so long I turned the engine off and began to count cars. I'm not sure how many had already passed when I started, but I lost count and interest at seventy-eight.

We could have had a poker game, read *War and Peace,* invented time travel or just aged gracefully by the time that million-car, five-mile-per-hour train finally passed. Now there was a good chance we would miss our flight.

My right foot filled with lead and I drove like Parnelli Jones (Google him if you don't know who he is), weaving in and out of traffic. When we hit the rush hour Pittsburgh city traffic, and still had about twenty miles to go to the airport, we both figured we would be stranded another night in the Pitts of Hell as we did the stop and go shuffle on Route 22.

Finally, a sign said, "Airport, next right," and I squealed tires turning off at high speed. Then came the rental car drop-off, running to check in, and finally running into the plane as the last two to enter.

As soon as we sat down, wiping the sweat from our brows, the stewardess closed the door and we began to taxi to the runway. John looked at me and began to say, "The only thing that could happen now is the plane will cra . . ."

"Don't say it!" I interrupted him. "Don't you say another word. I think YOU are the bad luck on this trip. Your negative mojo caused the car to break down too, so not another word out of you, especially about this plane." I was only kidding him, of course—I think.

Surprisingly, we arrived in Newark on time and surprisingly our bags were circling the baggage carousel when we got there. At this point we were a bit punchy due to the ridiculous events of the trip. The good news as we landed on time without crashing and our luggage was there. Our luck was changing,

Or was it?

It was cold and windy as we walked through the parking lot to my car and it was beginning to rain. We got to the car, tossed the bags into the trunk, and I remember thinking that the only thing that could happen now was that the car wouldn't start.

It didn't. The battery was stone cold dead.

Welcome home.

What happened to Allegheny? U.S. Air acquired it. Since they couldn't spell it either, they assigned it the U.S. Air name.

U.S. AIR aka U.S. AIRWAYS

Because of their record of eight fatal crashes from 1971 to 1994, many frequent fliers began to dub them U.S. Scare.

They have survived but I believe it is partially because they spent eight million dollars to change the name to U-S Airways. I guess it is not as easy to say U-S Scareways.

PIEDMONT AIRLINES

Piedmont flew the eastern corridor. They were popular in the south and I think the crewmembers were all descendants of Civil

War Confederate veterans. There was definitely a yee-haa, damn you Yankee, mentality on board.

This was the first airline that I experienced a male stew, or steward. Perhaps it was because most women did not chew tobacco and did not often scream "yee-haa" on an airplane.

I can't remember the plane type they flew, perhaps a 727 or a DC-8, but I remember it had a staircase that dropped down from the tail where the greeting bubba, dressed in a wrinkled, cruddy white shirt, with a rebel flag tie hanging opened around his neck, would say, "Hi, y'all, go on up and find yer-sef a seat."

Once on board I noticed the seats looked more like they were folding chairs placed there for a hog-calling contest. I was waiting for the stew-guy to offer me a piece of rope to "tie in" as they called it.

Back then I was a smoker and usually the last ten or twelve rows became the London fog section. Most everyone coughed and it was common to drop a hot ash on your new polyester suit-pants and damn near set your crotch on fire. This would add to the air pollution on board; burning polyester and crotch is very toxic. The very next row in front of the smoking section was breathing fresh air. No smoke went there, of course.

Meals were not available on these short-hop flights, but there were some amenities. Mr. Stew would stroll through the smoke & choke section offering a free four-pack of cigarettes made by one of the North Carolina based tobacco companies to promote the nicotine addiction. Additionally, you may have been lucky enough to be offered a stick of gum.

Now, the Union Jack flies half mast on the Island.

SHAMROCK AIR

Now this airline was an emerald jewel of the skies. This is the airline where First Class must have been invented. Top shelf all the way.

Ever heard of it? Ever see the big green shamrock adorning the tail of their fleet of plane? (Not a type-o. I said plane—singular.)

Probably not. I don't know how long it was in existence but it was far too long.

Shamrock flew out of New Orleans. I used them to fly from New Orleans to Hammond, Baton Rouge, and once to Houston's Hobby airport.

There was usually only one flight attendant on board and the flights were almost always more than half empty. Or, for you optimists, half full.

On one memorable flight I recall sitting in the last row of the plane, in the smoking section, of course. There were only a few other people in the back and only ten or twelve up front. On this particular aircraft, the seat backs could be folded all the way forward, which was a great idea. If no one was in the seat in front of you it was nice to flatten the seat-back, then you could put your feet up.

Once airborne and the smoking light was lit, a twenty-something stew came over to me, and the guy sitting next to me, and asked if either of us had a cigarette. Certainly, why the hell else would I be sitting in the smoking section?

I offered her one of my Marlboros. She took it, popped it in her lips, lit it and then, to my shock, she folded down the seatback in front of me and proceeded to sit cross-legged in her little stew skirt. I looked at the guy next to me and saw that he was beginning to blush.

My assumption was that to this girl the word *class* was only something she failed in the fifth grade.

While flicking her cigarette ash onto the floor, she appeared to be trying to take photographs of me through her white panties — if you get my drift. She talked incessantly about how she would eventually be getting a job with a *real* airline and getting away from this crumby one. Did she ever suspect that she was part of the cause that made this airline so crumby?

The guy next to me had a sheepish grin on his face the entire time and had little to say. When she said she had just interviewed with a really big airline up north, he asked which one.

"Piedmont," she said proudly.

She finished her cigarette and said, "Well, I guess I'll give those jerks up front a soda so they don't start ragging on me. You didn't want anything, did you?"

What a classy lady.

This flight was bound for Houston's Hobby Airport, but unknown to me, it was to make a stop in Lafayette, Louisiana for directions, gas and to drop off and pick up passengers.

Only two people got off. But the group that got on was very strange indeed. I guessed it was a large assembly of Cajuns going to a bluegrass festival in Houston. Straw hats, denim coveralls, lots of long beards, plaid flannel shirts and some homely women shuffled down the aisle. A strange collection of stringed instruments began to fill the overhead compartments. Many looked to be home made. One was a type of banjo made from an old cigar box.

The topper was the people who came on board carrying cages made from willow branches and tied together with twine. Chickens were the caged cargo. These were placed carefully in the overhead, and then the lid was slammed down into place causing a flurry of bucking and clucking. Perhaps this was the backup group.

During the flight, some of musicians took out their instruments and began to play. Even though the quality of sound was poor the talent was evident. I even found my foot tapping all by itself.

When we landed in Houston, ending this interesting trip, I thought the sideshow was over. But when the overhead compartments were opened the chickens were startled and began screeching and flapping their wings. The cabin began to look like a pillow fight was in progress. There were feathers flying everywhere.

One of the men opened the cage trying to calm the chicken and as you might expect, the chicken flew out and onto a seat. But the Cajun was fast. He swooped up the bird and stuffed it back into the homemade cage, leaving only a white chicken dropping on the seat.

Did you ever try to explain why chicken feathers were in your dirty laundry bag?

Shamrock Air is now pushing up clover somewhere near TWA.

***

NATIONAL AIRLINES

Did you know National became the first exclusively jet powered service in the United States? I flew this carrier only a few times to Florida. It must have been a good airline because I have no recollection of any incident flying with them.

Baby boomers will remember National was the airline that had an advertising campaign in which a cute blonde, brunette or redhead stew appeared on your TV screen and said, "Hi. I'm Beth. Fly me." This was a quite memorable ad campaign that sold stewardesses as sexy babes that you may have a chance with. However, it eventually pissed off the thin-skinned women that now make up the hard-core membership of the militant wing of the NOW organization. Humorless, aren't they? I guess I'm now on their hit list. Like I care.

Also, and I'm sticking my neck out here, I think it was also National that ran commercials in which a popular announcer would say, "Come on down! Be my guest." And some people took him up on the offer because they said it was at *his expense*, they were his guests. Needless to say, the commercial was pulled.

Speaking of pulling ads, in 1967 United Airlines ran TV commercials aimed toward businessmen's wives. The TV commercial used a little song that went, *Take Me Along If You Love-a-me*. It was used to try to get the guys to buy that extra ticket out-of-pocket. Road warriors went nuts because of the grief they got from their wives. United lost a ton of business and quickly changed the ad campaign.

National eventually did so well that they were merged with Pan American and the name dissolved in 1980. And as you know, Pan Am bit the dust later, taking with it the routes it got from National.

Another low fare airline based in Las Vegas, called themselves National Airline in the '90s. But they were short-lived and ceased operations in 2002. When they pulled the plug, they stranded thousands of passengers by canceling all flights without warning.

MOHAWK AIRLINES

They were a regional carrier. They had routes throughout New York and New England. I did not use them very often and I only remember that I didn't get scalped on the fares. (*Rim shot*)

FRONTIER

Not the Frontier that filed for bankruptcy in April of 2008, but the one from a number of years ago—the one that Peoples Express bought. They were one of the first not to use a tug to push them out of the gate. The pilot would just crank up the jets with reverse thrusters and back out of the gate under the aircraft's own power. But when fuel prices rose drastically it was back to the tugs.

Frontier was a no frills airline that I used when flying between Denver, Phoenix or Albuquerque. Frills, or not, I can attest they had some damned good pilots. Why do I say that, you ask?

While I was waiting to take off on a Frontier flight at Denver's old Stapleton Airport, the sky began to darken and a few huge droplets of rain began to smack loudly against the window next to where I was sitting.

The captain's voice came over the intercom and told the crew to get everyone seated because he wanted to get off the ground before the thunderstorm hit the airfield.

Before the storm? Okay then, so what were those quarter-sized raindrops began to splat on the planes fuselage like clear seagull crap?

In a few minutes we were backing out of the gate area, engines screaming, under power. When we were far away enough from the gate the pilot dropped the reverse thrusters and began a fast taxi to the beginning of the runway.

We were number one for takeoff. So once lined up with the centerline, the engines were pushed to full throttle. We raced down the runway as we began a thrilling flight to Albuquerque.

The 737 aircraft lifted off the ground and began to climb into the darkening sky.

As I looked out the window I saw that the rain was falling very hard now. It streaked across the plane's side windows in thick rippling sheets. The wind was picking up as well because the plane was bouncing, dipping and being literally tossed around by the weather.

Normally, this is no cause for concern. But we were only about four or five thousand feet off the ground and at the speed we were traveling; a simple dip could put us into the ground like a giant lawn dart. Sure, the altimeter may have said eight or ten thousand feet but remember, Denver is already a mile above sea level and the air is quite a bit thinner so it takes longer to gain altitude.

The ground didn't seem to be getting any further away as I could hear the engines straining to rise above the wind and weather. Seeing lightning in the not-so-distant distance, I guessed we didn't out run the storm by much—if at all. I also began to hear people starting to cry out each time the plane dropped a few feet and slammed into concrete hard air.

Now, I must say, I am not a white-knuckle flyer and never have been, but I found myself holding onto the armrests trying to keep centered in my seat and wondering if this plane was going to eventually punch through the frightening black cloud-cover still a good distance above us, or not.

I was looking straight out my window and suddenly the black ceiling was gone. Some sort of wind shear either pushed down on the left wing or pushed up on the right one, or both, because the plane was sideways and I was looking straight at the ground with gravity pressing me against the window.

Now, people were screaming loudly in utter panic, as I remained quiet, damned fool I am, squeezing the armrests and planting my feet solidly and uselessly on the floor, hoping this was only one of those pilot pranks. *Sure, that's what it is. I could imagine the pilot saying, "Okay you wimps back there, let's play LET'S SEE WHO DOESN'T PUKE."*

Unfortunately, it was no prank.

As my weight was leaning on the window on my left the plane began to shutter and vibrate noisily and somewhat violently as the pilot, probably screaming himself, throttled the engines forward and finally righted the plane back to a slight climbing angle.

The whole sideways episode maybe lasted a half-minute or so, or was it a lifetime? The plane was then dead silent except for the roar of the engines and some dripping sounds from the person two rows ahead that had wet their pants.

Everyone breathed easy but I heard no comments or conversation as I saw most people were wide-eyed and looking straight ahead as if in shock.

Finally, the pilot came over the intercom again and of course started with, "Well folks," and was that a quiver in his voice? "It's a little rough out there today so I'm going to ask the flight attendants to stay in their seats until we get above this weather. When we get to cruising altitude, I will turn off the seatbelt sign and cocktails will be on the house."

This time there were cheers in the plane. Free alcohol cures a lot of things.

When the flight attendants were up and about and getting drinks, my request was for two double scotches. I gulped them down quickly and also quickly got semi-drunk, but I felt a lot better.

The rest of the flight was either uneventful or I just was too drunk to remember. But I do remember staggering off the plane in Albuquerque and bouncing like a pinball off the walls of the Jetway. Some loss of balance was from good ol' Dewars but some was just getting my land legs back from that awful flight. I assumed this because it seemed everyone was playing pinball in the Jetway. Or, maybe they were as drunk as me.

Good pilot!

I hope he bailed out before Frontier hit the Island.

HOOTERS AIR

Now here is a real hoot—Hooters girls in the air. At least the current form of chubby, old, ugly, or a guy, got a somewhat decent upgrade. However, there were some officially trained flight attendants on board for the safety issues—like what to hang onto in case of a water landing. Now that's a no-brainer.

The Hooters Girls dress code was that of the restaurants' and it catered to golfers and men on leisure trips.

I never had the opportunity, or desire, for that matter, to book a flight on Hooter's Air. I'm not a golfer, you see. So I cannot comment if it was good or bad.

Hooter's Air was a short-lived venture. It began in March of 2003 and ceased operations in April of 2006. But it still does charters as of this writing. It sited rising fuel costs and lost revenues due the 2005 hurricane season as the reason for ceasing business. However, I think the real reason was they just wore the pair of front bumpers off all the planes during landings.

Chapter 4

Security

Security has always been the demonic curse to the business traveler. It is one of those necessary evils that add more stress to the already stressful everyday business dealings.

Before 9/11, most of the people who were responsible for our so-called security were mostly idiots. Now, I don't mean that in a demeaning way . . . or maybe I do. The pre-9/11 security crews loved the fact that they were "in charge," with a full level of Wyatt Erp syndrome. Many of these people had a lot of experience leaning against the wall while being patted down by police. So now was their chance to get at the *man* . . . the businessman, that is.

Despite their "look at me, I'm cool, I control you" attitude, I discovered you could easily distract them with humor, because they were about as bright as a dead flashlight.

A classic that sticks in my mind was the time when I was running very late for a flight. I checked in at the ticket counter and ran to security. I tossed my briefcase on the X-ray belt and passed through the metal detector without incident. As I went to retrieve my briefcase, a rather gargantuan woman, nearing the quarter-ton weight category, said, "Gotta see inside yo bag," as she tapped on my briefcase.

"Okay," I said. "Be my guest."

She fussed with the catches until I impatiently reached over and snapped them open for her. She began to rummage and peer into every small pocket and nook and she was taking her sweet time. After all, at five bucks per hour, might as well make it last.

I couldn't take it any more and said rather impatiently, "What are you looking for?"

Her reply was slow and simple. "I'm looking for something long."

"Honey," I said. "Your boyfriend ain't here so come on I've got to catch my plane."

With that, she laughed and said, "Ah ha! That's a good one." Then she shut my briefcase and handed it to me with her bloated paw and I was on my way.

***

For many years there was no intelligence, rhyme or reason for some of the things the security people did. Once I had a pencil and a pen. The pen was allowed but the pencil wasn't. Sometimes you needed to show a boarding pass, sometimes you didn't. I always carried a Swiss Army toolkit in my carry-on bag and even though it had a knife, among many other gadgets, it was never questioned. Never!

I always thought that this was a job for people who always wanted to be cops, or some other authority position, but either they couldn't get out of the fifth grade, or jail so this was the next best thing.

Then came September 11, 2001. This was a tragedy that would change the way we live and the way we travel, I believe for a very long time. Three thousand innocent souls lost their lives because some fanatics hate us and want to kill all of us for reasons only they and Professor Ward Churchill, and a few like him, seem to think is just.

We then were told to pay attention to color levels of threats: Red, orange, yellow and green, with red being the highest. Since we have been orange, one step away from the dreaded red for years, no one pays any attention to it any longer. We are told to be vigilant, and I certainly am. If I see an unattended bag I will report it, but usually it belongs to some dope that decided to leave his bag in a corner and go get a cup of coffee.

That fateful day began the demonic curse of all business travelers for a lifetime (or more) to come.

The old crew was to be replaced by the TSA, another bureaucratic arm of the U.S. government, short for Transportation Security Administration. Or was it replaced? In the beginning I started to notice the same faces now with different shirts—cleaner shirts—only because they were new.

Within the first year, it was discovered that many of the people *were* fifth-grade graduates, ex-cons, illegal aliens, or just plain idiots. Sound familiar? Wow, it took only a whole year for a government agency to figure this out. The good news is now we have upgraded our security personnel and equipment.

We even have informative video display messages as we approach the security line. Red circle symbols with the diagonal slash line to designate "NO." So, up pops a circle-slash with a knife depiction. Got it: No Knives.

Next is the circle with the pistol in it. Sure, No Guns.

But the kicker was the circle–slash with the cartoon style depiction of a round object with a lighted fuse sparkling on top. No Bombs! Who would have thought? Gosh, I always used to be able to bring a bomb before.

My guess is the *new* security sixth graders, who were much brighter than the previous fifth graders, designed those signs under a high paying government contract.

Recently, however, I noticed the bomb message has disappeared. I guess you can bring bombs on board planes again but not that nasty bottle of Poland Springs, or God forbid, hairspray, or shaving cream in a six once container.

If I were to create a hit list, that son-of-a-bitch Shoe Bomber would be at the top of it. Ever since he tried to light his Nikes we all have to trudge our smelly feet across a pathway and threshold of residue from other people's smelly feet, along with filth, bacteria, foot fungus, fecal matter and God knows what else just to get on an airplane.

Then came the underwear bomber. X-ray machines for scanning are good for seeing into you private parts but X-rays are also harmful. Pregnant women should not walk through those machines. I will not either. At my age I have had enough X-rays and do not need more cancer-causing radiation.

The naked views of passengers will be gawked at behind closed doors by the TSA. I can imagine some of the comments. Still, the security chiefs refuse to do what is needed — profiling. Old women, normal families and a multitude if road warriors with children will be treated the same or worse as the seventeen to thirty-five year old Middle Eastern man who fits the *profile.*

A comedian made a joke about if a terrorist inserting explosives in his anus and what we will all suffer after that. In truth, it is not at all funny because the TSA already wears rubber gloves. If that happens, I'm retiring.

If you're not in a hurry, you do not have to take off your shoes. Just tell them you can't due to religious reasons, or say you have medical feet deficiencies, (that's a big word for them) or just say, "I can't," then politely request to be hand scanned.

Once the "male or female assist" shows up, he or she will wand you for metal. And since you didn't set off the metal detector before, he or she is going to tell you your ankle is beeping, or your ass, or your chest.

Once, I saw a TSA guy wanding a circular pattern around an old bald guy's head. I couldn't figure that one out but this is your tax dollars at work with high tech equipment.

After the hand scan and pat-down you will be asked to remove your shoes so they can be brought to the belt for X-ray. Good.

Now your socks won't have little pieces of some mysterious sticky crap on them and it will be the TSA guy who has to carry your smelly, nasty-ass-from-wet-floor-in-the-restroom shoes to the belt, then back to you.

What bothers me most about airport security is the lack of profiling. Oh, my gosh! Did I say a dirty word? You can't do that! It's not politically correct.

To profile is to take historical, repeated pattern characteristics that pertain to a certain trait, appearance or action and compile them into a group of facts. Or, a set of characteristics or qualities that identify a type or category of person or thing. Or, a description of behavioral and personality traits of a person compared with accepted norms or standards.

When I see some eighty-year-old woman in a wheelchair or walker, who is forced to remove her leg brace so it can be inspected, or some poor old man who is being yelled at to turn his palms upward while he is being wanded for weapons, and because of his arthritis it would not allow the motion, I may comment to the TSA person, "Why don't you start profiling for terrorists and stop harassing American citizens? When did you ever see an octogenarian terrorist?"

The other thing is the random; *really bust your chops,* inspection. This is where, because you are a fourth generation German, Irish, Italian, etc. American, all gray-haired, white guy, you may be treated like a scum criminal terrorist.

My experience was in Orlando where there is a maze of inefficient security lines usually longer than the line for Disney's Space Mountain. You join the line and show your ID and boarding pass to the first security person and are allowed to enter the mob-scene. You then stand in a line that starts as one, then splits into several, only to join again as one where everyone pushes and fights for the next position. Sometimes, to reduce the chaos, they will direct us gray-haired white guys, a few middle-aged women and some octogenarians into the special "really bust 'em" line.

There were three of us that time in the hectic line of families finished with Mickey Mouse and his three-fingered cohorts. Two of us, are to be described as above as vanilla-looking gray-haired guys and the third darker skinned Italian guy had a dark beard who looked similar to some of the 9/11 wanted-list people. The "gray hairs" got to go to the concentration camp, death-march line that dragged on much longer than the chaotic original line. The beard was through and done and we were just rounding the corner wall which now exposed the extended screening area.

A TSA Nazi (and I mean that with all due respect) walked through the metal detector and over to me and commanded, "Boarding pass!"

As I handed it to him he snapped it out of my hand, looked at it, said nothing and poked it toward my face. So I snapped it out of his hand and said sarcastically, "Thanks for your courtesy."

As I always do, I put my watch and phone in my computer bag, and have no coins in my pocket. I wear the same belt with a small brass buckle, which almost never trips the metal detector. I wear glasses and there are some fillings in my teeth, but in short, I'm airport-metal-detector friendly.

Col. Klink-Himmler walked back through the metal detector and beckoned, with an attitude, to me to come through.

Of course the metal detector sounded its alarm and he then commanded me to remove my belt. I bet you thought you had to comply with their every wish. Pardon me, but you don't.

As I mentioned before I don't always remove my shoes. For example: I wear orthotics in my shoes and sometimes my feet kill me when walking on hard floors. Plus, there have been times when removing my socks and shoes at bedtime I would discover some sort of unidentifiable sticky glop either stuck to the sock, or worse, a flattened snot-like thing stuck inside the shoe. Therefore, if my feet are in pain or the floor is not clean and carpeted, I refuse to remove them and ask for the magic wand.

As a side note, my wife stepped bare-footed into a spot on the carpet where someone had just thrown up. She leaves her shoes on now.

You are still being cooperative by requesting that they scan you with a hand wand.

I also have this thing about being made to get undressed and additionally, with bursitis in my left shoulder causing pain to thread my belt behind me, I may have to drop my pants to do that. So I will refuse to remove my belt as I did this time. Sometimes this pisses them off because it becomes inconvenient for them, but that was too bad for this guy.

As I expected, this certainly did piss him off. So he asked again to see my boarding pass. I guess he thought it might have changed since the first time. And again he snapped it out of my hand, just as did I on the retake.

"Put your feet there, arms out, palms up," *you bastard,* he spat out to me.

It is my understanding that you are supposed to keep the wand a distance away from the body. But this guy was getting my ankles to beep as well as my back and my chest by sliding the wand over me as if it were a massage device. He would then pat down the beeping area. I began to think he just wanted to feel me up, the pervert. But when my wallet beeped, I sighed, "You've got to be kidding me."

He then took my wallet, which contained no metal whatsoever but a fair amount of cash. Sure, some of you pseudo-techs will say, "Oh, duh. But what about the magnetic strip on you credit cards?" Well, magnetic strips never set off any metal detector in—oh, about— eighteen hundred flights for me. How about you? Oh, yes, maybe I forgot the spare key in it? Well, I don't carry one.

He took my wallet and brought it back to the belt for X-ray and told me in his wonderful arrogant demeanor to "Get moving," and pointed to the conveyer where my bag and laptop had been sitting without me being able to watch it.

That reminded me of the TSA guy in San Francisco that was really pissed because I requested a scan in lieu of removing my shoes. When he was done, he told me to "beat it."

But then, while I was putting my shoes back on, there was another man requesting a hand scan. Now, he griped, "Jesus Christ! What the fuck is this?"

As I sat there tying my shoe I said to him, "If you don't like this job why don't you get one washing produce at the super market instead? You get paid by the hour and people like me and him"—I pointed to the poor guy who was next— "contribute to your salary every time we fly."

Surprised by what I said he replied, "I told you to beat it."

I got up and said politely, "Thank you for your courtesy and have a nice day." Then I turned to go to my gate.

But this jerk deserved a bit less polite remark. So for a second time I turned back to him and added the extension of "asshole."

I should have filed a complaint but I assume it would have been a waste of time.

Now, here in Orlando, as I snatched my bag from the end of the conveyor's rollers, a female TSA Nazi asked—no— demanded, to see my boarding pass, now for the fourth time.

I'm was then pissed-off to a red-face at this point. That was an appropriate time for the phrase, "Why don't you start profiling for terrorists and stop harassing American citizens." As expected, it did any good, and I stormed off to the terminal tram.

Just as I caught up with my gray-haired associate I remembered I never retrieved my wallet.

I got back to the conveyer and asked for my wallet and was told it was brought to the security desk a few seconds ago.

"Where's that?" I asked and was directed to a podium about fifty feet away.

As I approached, I saw a middle aged TSA woman with my wallet in her hand. It was open and she was not looking for any ID. She was leafing through and counting my money. Now, I was really pissed off.

"Hey! That's my wallet! Give to me!" I shouted at her.

Looking like the proverbial "caught-with-the-hand-in-the-money-jar" look, she said. "Oh—let me see your driver's license."

"It's in the goddamned wallet and the photo doesn't look anything like Lincoln, Grant or Jackson. Now, give it to me," I said angrily.

She immediately handed it to me without ever really knowing if it was mine since I didn't look even close to any of those guys on the bills.

***

My rules for their rules:

1. Wear the same belt each time you travel. One with skimpy metal buckle and preferably made of cast brass.
2. If you intend to take off your shoes, wear old, beat-up, stretched-out slip-ons. Note: Florsheim makes "airport friendly" shoes with no metal shank, even though you are supposed to take them off anyway. I wear the Comfortechs, Riva model. Very comfortable and an easy slip-on and off. So if you keep your shoes on, at least you won't be setting off the metal detector.
3. When you check in, or check your bag, put your phone, coins, keys, coins, pen and any foil wrapped items in your carry-on bag before going to the security line.
4. Don't bring liquids. Put them in your checked bag. But if you must, three once bottles maximum and all in a one-quart zip bag. Phoenix Sky Harbor and Dayton Airports and a growing number of additional airports will supply bags and booties. (They all should.)
5. Take off your coat, jacket or any over garment or hat. (Sweat shirt, vest, etc.) Just be sure you don't go to bare skin—guys, anyway.
6. Remove your laptop, video camera, DVD Player and place in a separate tub.
7. Order through X-ray: shoes first, electronics next, bag last.
8. Don't go through metal detector until all your items have gone through to X-ray.
9. Don't take your belt off unless you're a weenie or it is a large metal WWE championship belt.
10. If you remove your shoes, send them through X-ray first (See 7) so you can begin to slip them on right away and avoid stepping in any more snot-balls.

11. Keep your boarding pass in your back pocket or shirt pocket if it will fit and pull it out as you walk through the scanner. This pisses them off for some reason.

12. Since the Underwear Bomber's attempted attack, body X-ray machines have popped up at airports. As mentioned previously, I have been subjected to X-ray for many years for medical purposes and see no need to accept being subjected to any more cancer-causing radiation than necessary. You are within you rights to request a manual search as I do.

13. Remember, they are there for your safety, not to abuse you. But also remember, they are not there for you to abuse them either. You need to be cooperative and polite until you are being abused. So if someone is rude or nasty to you, tell him or her that they are acting inappropriately, or ask to see the supervisor. Oh, and the words "being an asshole" is normally an acceptable description in these cases.

Interestingly, a recent survey found that the TSA is now more hated than the IRS.

No surprise to me.

***

One of the good news items was that we frequent travelers can now sign up for the *Fly Clear* program.

They did a background check, took fingerprints and an eye scan. There was a fee but you would get through faster at security but not necessarily any easier. I had only used a few locations, such as Indianapolis, San Jose, and San Francisco and thankfully, at Orlando. What a pleasure not to have to stand in Orlando's torturous security line.

However, for financial reasons the concept ceased operations in 2009. Too bad.

Chapter 5

Delays and Cancellations

Most annoying, to the business traveler, is delays and cancellations and these are not isolated to just the airline industry. Cars, trains, busses and taxies, or anything that transports your from point A to point B, are all highly qualified to enhance the flow of your stomach acids. More Pepto Bismol—please.

Once the great aluminum bird finally does get to your destination it may only be just the beginning of another delay. An example is when you are waiting for the rental car bus and it is broken down at the exit of the rental car center and no other busses can get out taking its place.

Or when the broken down bus is towed out of the way and your are finally able to get your car and get on the San Diego Freeway from Century Boulevard in Los Angeles only to find the traffic is stopped dead all the way to Orange County.

So how do we handle that? The simple answer is, "Not well."

First, let's look at the airlines. There are only four official types of delays: weather, mechanical, crew being over-timed-out or anything else that does not fall into the other three.

Sure, you may ask, "What about ATC, or Air Traffic Control issued holds and delays?" Well, ATC delays usually fall into "weather conditions" at some other airports, which will slow things down for the entire country. Many times your plane will not leave the airport so there will be no wasted fuel by requiring your aircraft to circle while other planes are landing at a slower rate due to the weather. Personally, I hate it when I am on my way home and ATC makes my pilot do figure eights and circles in the sky to kill time before landing, for weather reasons. With thousands of planes in the sky at any given time I just want to go straight to the runway, land and not be one of those thousands of aircraft that air traffic controllers are trying to keep from colliding into each other in the sky.

The question has been asked, "What is a similarity between pilots and air traffic controllers?" The simple answer is if a pilot screws up, the pilot and passengers die. If the ATC guy screws up, only the pilot and passengers die.

***

Weather is the killer of hope that you will arrive at your destination on time, if at all. Weather is the root of the most dreaded *cancellation* and weather cancellations leave the airline no responsibility to you for anything, except maybe rebooking you for a later time, day, week, or month.

If the plane is delayed or canceled for a mechanical problem and you will be stranded at the airport for a considerable amount of time, usually you will get, if requested, a meal voucher. These are mostly for fast food places or for a dollar amount that is equal to fast food costs so don't get your hopes up for a decent meal on the house.

If the next available flight is the next day, you should get a hotel voucher as well. Again, don't expect a stay at the Ritz-Carlton.

A simple delay of an hour or two is usually tolerable, unless you have made the really stupid mistake of setting up the most important meeting of the year to begin an hour after you were to arrive in Chicago. And it doesn't matter if the flight was to be six hours or thirty minutes. If you are late, you look like an ass and blaming the airline is lame. It will only emphasize your own poor judgment and planning.

The simple answer to almost never being late for your meetings when you are leaving your home territory is to leave the day before. It simply gives you a twenty-four hour buffer zone. If your flight happens to be cancelled completely, you then have the opportunity to postpone your meeting with a full day's heads up to your customer or client.

If the delay or cancellation happens when you are on your way home, it may be frustrating, but not something that will ruin your career. However, it does take a toll on your tolerance, patience and stamina when, for example, you leave Huntsville at noon on your way to Newark via Houston and you arrive in Newark fifteen hours later only to find your luggage went to Phoenix.

Then, you take more time to fill out the baggage claim information and head for the escalator that is not working at 3:30 in the morning, climb the motionless steps and head for the monorail tram to get the bus to where you are parked, only to discover the train you just missed is running "one-track service" and that means this one train has to traverse the entire airport in one direction, then return to your location – about twenty-five more minutes to wait.

And, since the driver of the parking shuttle you called didn't see you at the bus stop, he went back to his base for a nap.

Eventually you arrive home at 6:00 AM, eighteen total hours after leaving Huntsville. But, the good news is you were just ahead of the morning rush hour.

All that thanks to Mother Nature for the thunderstorms in Houston—not an unusual happening there.

Eighteen hours is not a big deal. Eighty-two hours is my personal record. I know there are some lucky folks that are reading this and saying they can top it. My heart goes out to you.

I'm sure those who were scheduled to travel on September 11, 2001 were grounded for almost a week. I know. I was cancelled for a trip on September 14th that week but the airports only began to reopen limited service beginning September 16th.

My experience began on an early summer Asian trip. I had booked two round trips: one from Newark to Osaka, Japan, returning from Tokyo, and one from Osaka to Taipei, then Taipei to Tokyo. I used Northwest Airlines for the U.S. to Japan and EVA Air for Japan to Taiwan.

To return home I left my hotel in Taipei at six o' clock in the morning for a flight that got me to Tokyo in plenty of time to wait for my U.S. flight, which was at five-thirty local time that afternoon.

Everything was going well and on schedule.

The Northwest flight was a non-stop to Detroit where I would claim my luggage, clear U.S. Customs and immigration, recheck my bag and board another plane to Newark for about an hour and a half flight.

The flight arrived in Detroit about eighteen hours after take-off from Tokyo. Another few hours and I would be home after only about thirty-two hours of travel time. After I rechecked my bag I went again through security and finally boarded the plane bound for Newark, where we sat on the ground for another three hours before they canceled the flight. The reason: weather.

We were told that there were thunderstorms around Newark so I called my wife to tell her I was delayed. She said, "There's no storms here," and then consulted her beloved Weather Channel for verification. There were no storms on the radar, but how much confidence do *you* have in the Weather Channel?

My guess was, that at the time, Northwest had the worst record for on-time arrivals. So rather than be late, they would just cancel the flight. It was the last flight to Newark for the day. So on to the next line for rebooking.

Standing in this long, and getting-longer line, I recalled the time when I was trying to get home from Minneapolis. After a three hour delay before getting off the ground and about four hours flying around storms the pilot gave us a "Well folks ..."

and said Newark's radar tower was hit by lightning and the airport was closed. Syracuse was the alternate landing site but it was full of planes, so we were returning to Minneapolis.

While everyone was crowding around the agent's podium, pushing and shoving to yell at the poor guy, I headed for baggage and started hitting autodial buttons for the hotels in the area, only to discover that some big convention had all the hotel rooms sold out. I finally asked the person at the Holiday Inn if there were any outlying hotels he could recommend and he gave the number of an Holiday Inn Express about ten miles away.

It was after 1:00 AM and the desk clerk said he had rooms. I asked if they had a shuttle and he said they did, but not at this hour. I asked him if he was working alone and he told me there was another person still working the desk with him. Hmmm? "You wanna make fifty bucks?" I asked.

He did, and I got a ride and a decent room for the night while many slept on the floor at the airport.

There is nothing like a good night's sleep in a bed, a shower in the morning, and lucky me, I got a first class upgrade on the first flight out the next morning.

Remembering Minneapolis, I called 411 for the numbers of the usual hotel names that are seen around airports and quickly secured a room at a Marriot Courtyard.

Once I was rebooked for the next morning's flight I went to the shuttle bus for the hotels.

By the time I was on the bus I was hearing comments that all the hotels were full. Those poor people, some with children, were riding the bus to plead for a room at each hotel. Yeah, it's called survival of the fastest. I was getting too old for camping on concrete floors. Kids are built to do that. Besides, they love the adventure of airport camping.

The next morning I told the desk clerk I was not checking out. I figured I could call when I got to Newark and check out and just billed for the extra day—an insurance policy of sorts. It was the best idea I had that week because the next three flights that day were canceled for the same reason—weather.

The following day I executed the same hotel plan and it paid off again due to cancellations.

What I haven't mentioned yet is the fact that, sure I had a room, bed and shower, but no one had been allowed to retrieve their bags. So when it was resolved I was not going to make it home again that day, I wangled a deal for a half-day car rental with National. They are still my favorite because of this one manager who took pity on me and cut me a break for a half-day rate.

After getting directions to the nearest mall I bought new socks, underwear, jeans and two shirts. When I got back to my hotel room I was amazed how my sixty-hour-old clothes actually walked themselves to the trashcan and squeezed tightly and comfortably into the bottom. You can't know the feeling unless you have lived it. It was wonderful to put on fresh clothes.

The entire next day was the same as the previous. I was at the airport getting on planes or waiting in the boarding area only to be told the flight was cancelled. I still had possession of the room and my treasured clean underwear and fresh shirt in my computer bag.

The last flight was scheduled for 9:00 PM and we boarded on time. The flight finally did take off around midnight and arrived in Newark around 2:00 AM. My bag was already there. It had arrived perhaps a day or two before, routed in some fashion that obviously was not good enough to transport people.

I called the Marriott and finally checked out of my precious room.

By the time I rolled into my garage at home, eighty-two travel hours had elapsed—my record.

Hopefully you got the drift of rule number one for cancellations: Don't get all nasty and indignant with the airline personnel—get a room first!

Also, it is always a good idea to carry any required medications with your carry-on and if you are really good, an extra set of underwear and socks—clean ones, that is.

***

Traveling from Newark to Fairbanks, Alaska via Seattle had an unusual combination of all three delays.

The Newark outbound flight was pending serious weather delays but was able to get off the ground only about an hour late. Usually the pilot can make up this time in the air by getting approvals for alternate routing. You know, like flying straight to Seattle instead of zigzagging across the country.

So the first delay was weather.

When we deplaned in Seattle I went to the schedule-monitors and looked for the flight to Fairbanks to see what gate I needed to go to. Nothing was listed for the flight number. Since these monitors were for all airlines I thought perhaps the ones for *Alaska only* would show the gate information.

I then trekked off to the Alaska Airlines terminal only to find their monitors did not list the flight either.

Asking a snooty little girl at one of the gates, I was told, "The flight is delayed at least two and a half hours."

"That is not what I asked," I replied. "I asked what the gate number was."

She told me Gate 26 so I walked there and sat down.

The reason for this delay was that the inbound flight was held up due to weather; at least at this time.

When the plane finally arrived about five hours later it was announced there was a mechanical problem as well—something with the rudder pedals. That made me recall the "rudder problems" with the Alaska planes a while ago where the rudder failures of their MD-80s were flying them into the ocean.

After an hour or so, it was announced that this plane was not going to fly today but no fears—they had another aircraft.

We were sent to Gate 9 on the far side of the terminal to wait for the plane, which was already there, to take off so they could tow *our* plane into its place. That took about an hour.

Finally, cheers from the passengers as a plane was slowly pulling up to the ramp.

The crew, who was also waiting to leave for as long as long as all the passengers, then boarded the plane. It wouldn't be long now.

It caught my eye when I noticed the canopy on the end of the Jetway where it covers the entrance to the aircraft was being retracted. I then saw a maintenance person outside appear and stretch on tiptoes so as to peer into the cockpit. This was not a good sign, It looks like another mechanical issue.

After a minute or so of peering, she left the Jetway and came to the podium at the gate and announced the aircraft had a cracked windshield and it was unknown at this time if it could be repaired for this flight. We would be updated as soon as possible. Round two had begun.

About an hour and a half later it was announced the windshield was okay. Strange, I was watching the plane the whole time and I saw no one new go into the plane and no one did anything to the outside of the windshield. I assumed the pilot had some spare duct tape or one of the flight attendants had some nail polish or crazy glue handy and the job was done from inside the cockpit.

Okay. Good news. I guess we would board soon—not.

The next announcement was that the crew was now "timed-out" and was not allowed by FAA rules to fly.

So now you know the third reason for delays: timing out.

Pilots can work for fifteen hours on domestic flights. That includes flying time and ground-waiting time. So when passengers are delayed, so is the crew that flies and serves them.

This Fairbanks flight was to be about four hours from Seattle and if the crew began the flight they would time out sometime during the flight.

So off comes the crew and it took another two hours to get a fresh crew out of their personal off-time and to the airport.

Total time elapsed, Newark to Fairbanks, was twenty-four grueling hours.

***

What if you miss your flight because you got a flat tire on the way to the airport, or you overslept, or you were flying on Southwest out of Las Vegas on a Sunday afternoon after the largest trade show in the country and the check-in lines were outside in the street from one end of the terminal to the other, then snaked around inside the terminal as usual? Yes, this happens occasionally in this glamorous career.

Now you will be delayed due to your own mistake or happenstance and the airline owes you nothing. However, as long as you check in within two hours of your original flight time, or at least call the airline; they must book you on one of the next available seats at no penalty in fare or other. Remember, "available" seat does not guarantee you will get on the next flight.

But, if you decide not to show up and do not at least call the airline to reschedule your flight, your ticket will be declared "of no value" which simply means you are screwed when you go to use it. You will have to purchase a new ticket and at the current fare, which will be about the same as the cost of a good, high-end used car.

I made this mistake once when I was returning from an Asian trip to Los Angeles, and then I was supposed to return to Newark from L.A.

Arriving in L.A. on that Saturday and realizing I would be leaving Newark again on the next Monday for a trade show in Las Vegas, I decided to scrap the flight to Newark and bought a Southwest ticket to Vegas to stay at the company's townhouse. This would allow me to rest up and readjust to the sixteen-hour time difference from Taiwan to Pacific Time and be fresh on Monday for setting up the booth at the Las Vegas Convention Center

Since I did not advise the airline that I would not be leaving Newark on Monday for Las Vegas on the first leg of that ticket, the ticket was declared "of no value" by the airline.

I discovered this when I tried to return from Las Vegas on the back half of the ticket that they canceled. The agent looked at me with both disdain and sadistic pleasure when she informed me I was now officially airline screwed and she was glad. (The bitch).

After some arguing and attempted reasoning I became somewhat perturbed, maybe even a bit nasty, and finally demanded to speak to her supervisor.

I told the supervisor my story, showed him the confirmation and receipt for my ticket purchase, showed him my Platinum Elite card imprinted, "Member Since 1986," to prove what a loyal customer I was, and then threw myself at his mercy. It worked. I got my ticket reinstated and flew off to back home at no additional fare. But I was lucky.

Now here is a tip. Just so the next guy that makes the same mistake doesn't get told to dig deep into his wallet, you need to commend and thank the person, in writing, for the favor. After all, they did not have to go out of their way to bail your sorry ass of your screw-up.

Be sure to get his or her name and write the airline, commending them for their patience and understanding and that *they* and other employees like them are the reason you continue to fly with that particular airline. It is good for the person's record and in all honesty, it made me feel good to express my appreciation.

Now, as for the first nasty person that basically told me to stuff it—I hope she pees herself in public, then slips and falls on her ass in the wet spot. No mercy there.

***

What if you open your eyes and realize it is 9:30 in the morning and your flight was at 6:30 and you are over the two-hour limit?

Get on the phone immediately with the carrier and when the agent says, "Hello, this is Jennifer. How may I help you?" you need to be very humble and a bit panicky and reply, "Oh, hi Jennifer. God, I hope you can help me. I'm in deep trouble here. I need to be in Kansas City by this evening and the hotel didn't give me a wake-up call and I can lose my job if this blows up and [note the rambling] I can't believe they did this to me and I don't know what to do and my boss is going to kill me and . . ." You get the drift.

Immediately Jennifer takes control and tells you to calm down, gets your name and information and begins her magic on the computer, coming to the rescue of the poor idiot on the other end so he doesn't lose his job. Usually, you'll get on one of the next flights that day, albeit in a middle seat. But you will usually get there on the same ticket and fare or with a minimum of penalty cost.

Now, if you get Clyde, the bastard who hates his job and wants to see you get screwed, hang up and just call back until you get a Jennifer type.

**

This one is tricky: you show up on the wrong day for your flight. Yes, I have done this a few times.

Usually it is a mistake in dates done by your travel agent or an office assistant who booked the incorrect date for your travel. And the other idiot, you the traveler, didn't check the dates on the ticket. So there you are, trying to check in and the agent tells you this ticket is for tomorrow, or worse, yesterday.

"Tomorrow" is the better of the two. These will usually only cost you a change fee, which could be one hundred fifty dollars, go on standby for that flight and you will suffer the middle seat torture for a few hours. Occasionally, you might get banged with a fare change, but you will usually get on the planned flight. If the fare increase if out of sight, you will either have to bite the bullet or change your schedule and come back tomorrow—not an easy task.

The "yesterday" scenario can be difficult to resurrect. Go back to the previous information when your ticket has no value and talk to the supervisor. And remember: if it was you that booked the wrong date, never admit it. Be the victim. This is a life crisis, so get all the pity you can create. After all, you are a sales person, aren't you? If you can't sell yourself and your line of bullshit, even in personal situations, forget the flight, go home and get a job sprinkling produce at the super market.

***

One day at the office I received a call from the company's largest customer telling me that there was a problem with one of the connectors my company sold to them. Since this customer bought millions of units from me I wanted to be at their facility the next day to solve the issue, or as we say, "Put out the fire."

I asked my assistant to get me onto a flight to San Juan and a hotel room for later that day.

She booked me on a 6:30 flight that evening so I went home, put tomorrow's clothes into a carry-on bag and headed for the airport.

The flight boarded on time but after an hour sitting on board, the passengers were asked to get off the plane because there was a mechanical issue that needed to be fixed. Thankfully, the aircraft door had not yet been closed. If it was, we may have had to sit in the plane while they hunted for the rubber bands and a screwdriver and then did the repair, which caused us to be four hours late.

The flight took off at about the time it was supposed to arrive in San Juan: 10:30 that night. This got me into San Juan after two in the morning.

I had never been to Puerto Rico before and I was not familiar with the airport or its procedures. When I went to the rental car counter I panicked because there was no one there at that hour. The lights were out but as I got close-up to it, I saw a hand-written sign with a phone number. I called the number on the sign and a woman told me to go to a specific door, turn right and walk until I see the rental car lot. She would be waiting for me; she had been waiting for me for the last four hours.

Sure enough, after a fairly long walk in the steamy, humid night, I saw that all the rental companies shared the same small lot. I then saw a woman waving at me.

She directed me to my car and I asked her for directions to the San Juan Marriot. Her English was not very good but I got the gist of it about getting on some road, go six exits, get off and bare right; that was it. It sounded simple.

It took me a few circles around the airport to find the exit and finally I was on my way. Understand that it was two-thirty in the morning, I had never been there before, I had no map, it was dark so I could not even establish landmarks and I was counting down six exits which are nothing more than side streets to the two lane elevated street that I was on. Finally number six came into view and it was a diagonal ramp off to the right.

As instructed, I kept to the right and it put me back onto a ramp that brought me back to the elevated street I just came off. Oh well, no problem, I'll just get off the next exit, turn back around and try it again. Or, so I thought.

As I later learned, bear right meant to make a hooked, almost U-turn off the ramp and head the opposite direction on the street parallel to the elevated road. The hotel was only about a block away. Who knew?

At the next intersection I turned off expecting to be able to get back on to the road in the opposite direction. But this was not the case. I was now headed off at a right angle to my exit on another highway and there were no apparent exits in sight.

I continued for several miles until I saw an exit coming up on my right. Unfortunately, this exit did the same thing: it put me onto another road without any means to turn around.

This happened twice more and I was so lost and so turned around, I was hard pressed to have any clue as to which way I needed to go, so I made a few illegal turns by crossing over medians just to go back the way I came.

Finally, getting off an exit that I thought was close to where I went wrong brought me into a neighborhood that I surmised I shouldn't be in. My clues were: it was three o' clock in the morning and the streets were crowded with clusters of rowdy teens, tough looking groups of older men, and a quite few ladies of the evening walking around strutting their stuff.

The only running vehicle on the street other than mine was a police car, which had stopped so the two officers could to speak to some of the rowdy teens. Thank God—cops.

I pulled alongside the police car and asked if they spoke English—they did.

"Can you tell me how to get to the San Juan Marriot?" I asked.

After a few questions to me asking if I knew where this or that was I told the cop I didn't know where anything was and I'd been lost since I left the airport.

He took pity on me and said to follow him and he took me right to the entrance of the hotel.

I thanked the officers, parked the car and went inside to finally check in.

Since I needed to be in Aguadilla the next morning by about ten and it happened to be on the opposite side of the island, I was only going to get about three hours sleep as it was. But when the desk clerk informed me that at midnight my room guarantee was expired and they gave away my room, I was about to go ballistic.

"You're kidding." (*You damned prankster*) "No! No! You can't do this to me. You have to give me a room," I told him.

"Sorry sir, we don't have any more rooms," he said with an air of superiority.

I looked around the spacious lobby, then back at the clerk and said, "You see that sofa over there?"

He nodded to the affirmative.

"Well I'll tell you what, pal. Either you get me a room or I'm sleeping right over there—and I sleep naked," I told Mister Important.

A slight look of fear came to his expression as he told me he'd see what he could do. I guess the thought that he would have to deal with that for the night was enough to put the fear of Bob into him.

He picked up the phone and had a short conversation in Spanish. He then hung up and returned to me and said, "Okay, sir. Do you know where . . .?"

"No. I don't know where *anything* is. I am not driving any more tonight and I am not getting lost because you sold my room. Wherever this is, *you* get me there and I am not paying for a taxi," I firmly told him.

The taxi dropped me off at 4:00 AM at a very nice, high-end hotel in Old San Juan. To this day, I never had any idea what the name was nor did I care at that point.

When I arrived in the lobby the sleepy clerk was ready for me and I signed the register, got my key and was finally ready to crash for the night. Before leaving the lobby I asked for a 6:30 wake-up call. Wow, a whole two and one half hours sleep, then off to the other side of the island.

The room was called the *Gloria Vanderbilt Suite* and it was incredible. There was a large living room, full-sized dining room, a huge bedroom with a veranda over-looking the ocean and a bathroom that was big enough to host a party for twenty-five people. But I would spend the next two hours and fifteen minutes in it with my eyes closed. What a shame.

I awoke to the sun glinting between the slits of my shuttered windows. Squinting to see what time it was I realized it was almost nine o' clock. The desk never set my wake up call and now I was in trouble.

Springing out of bed and directly into the shower I hurried as fast I could to get dressed and out the door.

When I got the front desk, a different person was working there. I complained about the non-wake up call but it fell on deaf ears. Not even a "sorry" was offered to the pauper who was messing up the sheets in this exclusive place and they were probably only getting paid a pittance for the room from the Marriot.

"Please call a taxi for me," I said. "My car is at the Marriot."

I waited for almost a half hour for the taxi and I was getting nervous about how late I would be for my meeting which was supposed to be to smooth things over and not to make them worse.

This experience happened in 1998 about a month after Hurricane Georges devastated the island of Puerto Rico. Consequently, many phone lines were still down and there was virtually no cell service or even pay phone service. So I could not call the customer to advise them that I was delayed but still coming. How embarrassing.

After a few wrong turns I was finally on the road to Aguadilla and after about an hour and a half of driving, well over the speed limit, I arrived at the huge industrial complex on the northwestern side of the island.

When I told the receptionist whom I was scheduled to see and was very late for the appointment, she informed me he had already left for lunch. Things were still getting worse.

When my contact returned from lunch and I apologized and explained what had happened, he was sympathetic to my plight and was appreciative for the trouble I had put myself through to react immediately to the problem. So the bad thing was actually becoming a good thing.

We concluded our business to a positive end and he then offered me a plant tour. Looking at my watch I had to decline because it was already 2:30 PM and my return flight was at 5:15.

Speeding as fast I could without causing havoc, driving through a blinding tropical downpour and making another wrong turn as I neared the airport, I eventually got on the plane with no more than fifteen minutes to spare.

Of course, due to a few thunderstorms in the area the flight was delayed.

But, all in all—it was no problem; just another day—another delay.

***

One last thought: When traveling in a foreign country on a foreign airline, all bets are off if you are the one who screwed up. You can try some of the tactics, but the rules are different and sometimes, just being an American may work against you. So don't be the *Ugly American* by copping an attitude. You need to be as nice and as humble as possible to try to gain some sympathy and cooperation. Then, expect to get screwed anyway.

In serious cases you may need to get the assistance of the local U.S. Consulate. Therefore, it is a good idea when traveling outside the U.S. to have those numbers handy.

As for a last, last thought, be sure to keep your passport safe, because you are not going anywhere without it. As a precaution, make two enlarged photocopies of the photo page with the passport number on it and keep one in your carry on bag and one in your checked bag. This will allow for a faster replacement from the U.S. Consulate if your passport is lost or stolen. Write the local consulate's phone number on the passport copy as well.

Chapter 6

You Sick Puppy

One of the worst things that can happen to you is to become ill when traveling. If you have an obsessive dedication to the job, or you are the eternally optimistic that "you'll be okay in a while," many times you will still strive to carry out your commitments even though you feel like you are dying. Just be certain that you are not.

***

The year was 1990 and I had been working for a wire and cable manufacturer as head of the connector division. I was solicited by this company and was eventually hired to start this division about five years prior.

The job had me traveling all over the United States and Taiwan. I was working sixty to ninety hours a week and was on the road most of the time trying to get the connector products running strong.

The biggest task I had to overcome was to convince the one hundred and thirty sales people and reps that they should sell connectors. For some odd reason, people in the wire and cable industry did not want to add to their sales numbers and sell accessory items. I called it a "cable mentality." That is where the thought process was, *why should I sell this stinking two dollar connector when I can sell a fifty dollar roll of cable?*

My answer was, because for each piece of cable that is cut from that roll there is a connector at each end, and they plug into another connector.

I even touted an example where the Atlanta branch of the company sold $8,000.00 worth of cable and $12,000.00 worth of connectors to use on that cable. That still didn't instill interest in the connectors. So I resolved that if it had to do with connectors, either I, or my huge staff of two people, did the job, or it didn't get done.

In late March of that year I had an important meeting in San Jose with one of the worst purchasing people I have run across in my career. He was one of those self-centered sons of a bitch that thought the world revolved around him— cocky, arrogant, abrupt and a downright rotten bastard. Aside from that, he was an asshole, too.

After working more than a year to get my product specified and approved by their engineering department, it took months to get a meeting with the king of all purchasing managers.

The meeting was scheduled for a Wednesday morning so my plan was to fly to San Francisco Airport on Tuesday, drive to San Jose and do the meeting on Wednesday. I would then return home on Thursday because I had to give full day training seminar on Friday.

The training seminar was one that I was to give to my company's national sales staff, reps and distributors at a hotel's conference center at Newark Airport. Maybe this time they would realize the dollars they could earn by increasing their sales in the connector product's line—optimistic fool that I was.

For a couple of weeks I hadn't been feeling very well which I diagnosed as extreme stress due to the heavy travel schedule and long working hours I was keeping.

When I arrived in San Francisco I called a friend of mine in San Mateo and he invited me to his house for dinner that evening. Then, I checked into my hotel and prepared myself for the next day's meeting with the King, then went to visit my friend and his wife.

It was a nice relaxing dinner but I was feeling bloated and had indigestion from what was a light dinner. I assumed the traveling and the anticipation of the next day's meeting was stressing me a bit and causing some indigestion, and yes, I slugged a shot of Pepto.

The next day the meeting with Mister King of Jerks was a disaster. No matter what I said the wise-ass, rat-bastard buyer (and I *do* mean that in a bad way) argued and disputed it. I would prove and substantiate what I was saying and he would just say. "I don't believe it." I would say he was one the biggest morons in the industry I have experienced – perhaps he *was* the biggest, and if someone hasn't killed him yet, he probably still is.

Nothing was going right and I was feeling pretty bad both mentally and physically so I closed the meeting by saying, "Look, there is nothing more I can say or do for you. Your engineering likes the product and they approved it, we can exceed the cost expectations you have, we can deliver as required and we have agreed to your sixty-days terms of payment. Why don't you mull it over and we can speak on the phone on Monday? I'll set up a conference call with you, your chief engineer, my regional and local managers, the vice president of my company and me. You can decide then if this is acceptable or if any other questions come up, there will be someone on the line that can answer them. Okay by you?" *Ya bastard!*

I went back to the hotel to unwind and to try to calm down and relax. That SOB had me worn to a frazzle and I felt awful.

Lying on the bed watching the TV news I decided to go get something to eat.

Just as I was ready to leave, the hotel operator called and said there was a fax for me at the front desk. I told her I would get it later as I was on my way out and was going out the back door where I was parked.

When I returned from dinner I had forgotten the fax until I got upstairs so I went back down and got it.

When I got back to my room it felt like I could hardly breathe. My stomach felt strange and I had a raspy feeling in the side of my chest, along the left side.

Still undaunted, I threw my bag on the bed, and with great difficulty began to toss my things into it.

Socks in . . . need to rest. Shirt in. Oh, God, I need to lie down, and so it went until I was packed. I couldn't recall ever feeling worse.

I went to sleep and awoke at 4:30 AM with the wake-up call. I felt a little better, but not much.

Fortunately, the gate to which my flight was assigned was a very short walk so I didn't have far to carry my shoulder bag and briefcase. There were no wheel-bags back then except the ones that were starting to appear tagging along behind flight attendants.

I slept the entire five and one-half hours on the flight to Newark and when I awoke, I felt a lot better. Not perfect, but compared to the previous night, I was great.

The seminar went well on Friday and I was able pull off a good session but something still was not right with me. The raspy pain inside my chest just under my armpit was getting worse. It felt like a cheese grater sliding around in there.

That weekend, one of my daughters had me toting her things to her college dorm room. Each trip from the car to the room was getting tougher and tougher. I was out of breath hauling boxes of her belongings a few feet out of the elevator and down the hallway.

On Monday I went to the doctor. He told me it was stress, as I thought, but as a precaution gave me a chest X-ray and prescribed a medication to help relax me. He said it would take about a week to start working. Chest X-ray?

Tuesday I took off and went fishing and discovered I couldn't climb up a low bank without needing a rest to catch my breath. I quit and went home.

I took the following Monday off again to rest and hoped to feel better. But by the next day I called the doctor and told him the medication was not working and if anything I was worse. I was still having those raspy pains below my armpit, more difficulty breathing, and a shooting pain every once in a while down my left arm. Something was definitely wrong.

He told me to double the medication and I said, "No. I think I'm having a heart issue."

I guess since I was only in my early forties he assumed I was being a paranoid fool for telling him my body was telling me something different than he was. So he got pissy with me and he told me to come on in and he would do an EKG if it would make me feel better, but to get there soon because he wanted to go home by one o'clock that afternoon.

With the EKG hooked up, I was having another heart attack in his office. The first one was when I left my heart (attack) in San Francisco. Then, I left the doctor's office in a mobile intensive care ambulance and a week later, I had a quadruple bypass.

Now for the good news. The day I was carted off to the hospital, Mary and I had an appointment to go to a session for quitting smoking. We were to get an acupuncture procedure where they stick some sort needle or staple-like device in your ear and when you want a cigarette you just tweak the thing and supposedly, you remain smoke free.

Well, we missed the session and saved $150.00 and still quit! Isn't that great? I saved all those bucks.

Interestingly, this was the beginning of a significant turning point in my career.

Unknown to me at the time, but I had a suspicion, the company I was working for was having some financial problems.

The original owner was retiring and in order to help maintain the cost of his yacht and its full time crew of four, he decided to sell the company. A group of British investors purchased the company but unknown to them, a great deal of the inventory value was worthless except for perhaps scrap.

I was told to add one million dollars of inventory a year earlier and I strongly suggested we did not do that. I told the CEO it was not needed to put that much into stock, especially since the market was declining in one particular series of product. And I certainly did not want to have him come back to me later and ask why we weren't moving that product out of inventory.

Since, at the time, I had no knowledge he was beefing up numbers so he could negotiate a higher price for the company, I continued to resist until he ordered me to, "Just do it!"

The bad part of the sale of the company was that his son became the new company's president and was to run the company.

Now here was one guy who had it all—that is, a silver spoon in his mouth from birth and a smaller silver spoon up his nose snorting that white powder that got him through the day. But that doesn't make him a bad person, only an idiot. What made him a bad person was his little rich boy attitude when he tried to dominate and intimidate people who worked for him and his total lack of concern and respect for anyone, including his wife and family members.

Since I reported directly to his father, I was then to report to him after the sale was completed. I could hardly wait.

It wasn't long before I had a run-in with him and since he was a know-nothing spoiled brat, I quickly put him in his place and didn't care about the risk. I had principals and I would not give them up for someone like this guy. He was shocked and perhaps a little afraid, because someone stood up to him, but it didn't earn me any respect because he respected no one; however, it allowed me to be left alone to do what needed to be done.

The Britts drained cash from the business before they realized they had bought a pig-in-a-poke and with Snotty boy at the helm, this business was teetering on financial ruin.

While lying in the hospital waiting for my surgery, infused with a nitro glycerin drip in my veins, and occasionally a nurse or doctor would run into my room ready to give a couple of jolts, and I don't mean of Dewars. As ill as I was I was still thinking about some of the deals I had going and hoping that my staff of two were doing what was necessary in my absence.

During that time and even after I returned home, the people in the company were great. They called Mary, sent cards, called me and they were truly concerned, except for Snotty boy . . . never a call or a card from him.

I did receive three days sick pay and a week after I returned home I received a letter from the Spoon-Man telling me that since I was not driving my car, he was suspending my car allowance. Nice, I guess I was supposed to suspend paying the lease company. A nasty prankster he was.

Then, about two weeks after I had returned home from the hospital, my wife answered the phone and told me Snotty was on the phone.

I figured it was about time he called to see if I was alive. Wow, was I ever wrong.

I said hello and all hell broke loose on the other end of the line. He was screaming incoherently about some defective material from a customer that I returned to stock and denoted in the inventory list, "Do Not Sell – Defective – Pending RTV" (Return to vendor).

Listening to him rant, I knew now for sure the company was in trouble with money. He was teed off because this was forty thousand dollars he couldn't use as collateral for loans, but I played ignorant to that.

Visualize a guy that was working sixty to ninety hour weeks, (stress) traveling constantly, (stress) is two weeks out of major surgery having a healing incision on his leg from the ankle to the groin, an incision from the top of the belly to the top of the sternum, stainless steel bailing wire holding his cracked sternum together, and his boss, who never once said, "Hey, how you feeling?" or "Glad you're OK," (More stress) and is screaming at his dedicated employee.

No. I refused to accept more of this stress, not now. So I politely told him never to call me at home again, and that I may not be in good shape now, but if he ever talked to me like that again, he will be very sorry. Then I hung up.

But back to the point of more good news: When I did get back to work I received a call from a buyer from a large company that was ready to give me some business that I had been working on two years prior.

He was kind of a tough-nut guy, but a decent guy and he pushed for me to get into the engineering department to try to get my products approved and now the effort was about to pay off.

Or, was it?

The order would amount to fifty thousand dollars, but I had to tell him I couldn't accept the order. This was due to the fact that the company still had no financial resources and would not be able to issue a letter of credit, or LC as it is called, to the vendor in Taiwan.

He immediately got angry saying, "Jesus H. Christ. I went out on a limb for you and now you're going to make be look bad. Shit! Why not?"

Rather that tell him the story I asked if I could call him back the next day and he agreed.

That evening I called the manufacturer in Taiwan. I had a good trusting relationship with the owner so told him about the order and asked him if he would trust me personally. Understand, I didn't have a dime and with some uncovered hospital bills, I wouldn't have the proverbial two nickels to rub together for quite some time and I was going way out on a limb. But I knew this customer would pay in ten days.

When it was agreed I would pay after I received payment for the material I had the plan wrapped up.

Some years earlier I had a part time woodworking business—custom furniture, unique clocks and tables, and the like, made from exotic woods. I retired the business due to not having time to stay ahead of demand and keep up with the full time job and travel schedules. This business had a registered business name, with a tax ID and a still valid bank account in the name of Bomar Creations. Bo, for Bob and Mar, for Mary.

The next day I told the buyer I would accept the order but he had to issue it to a company called Bomar.

It was done. My life would turn around and take a different path that would prove to be a risk well worth taking.

Shortly thereafter I resigned from Snotty Boy's company with a business backlog of two hundred thousand dollars, and then incorporated as Bomar Interconnect Products and this would be my last career change until retirement.

You may ask, "What about the stress of running a business?"

Good question.

I coined the explanation, "I was tired of working for jerks. The more you did the more they wanted and the less they appreciated it. So if I'm going to work for a jerk, it may as well be me. Because I can live with him . . . and I do."

As far as stress goes, one does need to manage that as you would manage the business. So far, I've been pretty good at it.

***

Fortunately, nothing that serious has happened again. (At least at the time of these words) But Dallas, Cleveland, Detroit, Boca Raton, San Jose and Taipei have afforded me the experience of some wonderful food poisoning.

On the surface you may say that the six times in all those years is not that bad. But if you have never suffered the woes of food poisoning you have no right to think that. Considering the thousands of meals I have eaten in restaurants I figure your chances are that the food is 99.98% safe or at least your body will handle simple bacteria without your noticing. But that .02% can really spoil your day and night. Vomiting, diarrhea, with fever and chills added, camping on the bathroom floor wrapped in a bedspread is not a happy time, especially knowing you have a full day's work ahead of you tomorrow and you intend to push ahead come hell or high water.

The Dallas event came from a salad bar at a Steak & Ale with dinner. I did wind up losing the entire next day mainly because my sales rep, with which I had dinner the night before, was also sick.

Cleveland, I can't say for sure how I picked up the bugs but since I know I didn't lick any doorknobs, chicken cutting boards or toilet seats, it might have been just from breathing the air.

Detroit's gastrointestinal issue actually came from a hamburger, with lettuce, that I had in Manchester, New Hampshire earlier that day. Thank you Wendy.

I was feeling queasy when my plane landed in Detroit so I figured it was best to perhaps have only a bowl of soup for dinner. Big mistake.

Someone told me soup is usually all of the day old, left-over food tossed into a pot and made into today's salt saturated sludge, then mixed into a greasy lubricant for additional stomach disorder. I don't know if that is totally true in all cases but the beef barley soup I ordered started to feel like it was defying gravity in my stomach at about the fifth spoonful.

The rest of the night I was as sick as a dog that had eaten antifreeze meatball.

In the morning I forced myself to do an abbreviated, 7:30 AM meeting to a bunch of sleeping sales people who could care less about me or what I was saying. The bummer was I was doing this meeting as a favor for another product manager from another product group in the cable division. Not even my product. I then made one sales call and went back to my hotel.

I dozed off and woke up at two in the afternoon—two hours after my flight had taken off. I had to do some fast-talking to the airline to get a seat on another flight later that day but arrived home about six hours late.

Boca Raton: it was a salad bar again. It is difficult to interview a potential new rep when you want to puke, but I didn't. Fortunately, the diarrhea waited until I got back to my hotel and just kept me up all night.

San Jose: a Caesar Salad at a Hyatt. The salmonella or giardia tainted Caesar Salad I ate in San Jose caused a frustrating schedule change. The salad was for lunch and by dinnertime I was getting pretty sick.

Again, I sat on the bathroom floor, shaking with chills, praying to the god of vomit, Rooork, and occasionally switching positions for opposite reasons. This was how I spent the most of the night.

The next morning, a distributor salesman was supposed to pick me up at 5:30 AM at my hotel in San Jose and we were going to drive to Grass Valley, CA, which was a couple of hours away. This was an important trip I had planned and I did not want to cancel it. But I called his cell phone at five o' clock and told him the trip was off for me. I still was running to the bathroom periodically and I looked and felt like something the cat dragged in.

Additionally, now I had to cancel my flight from Sacramento to San Diego for later that day and try to re-book my San Diego leg out of San Jose instead. Luckily, I got one for six o' clock that day.

I called the hotel desk and informed them I was willing to pay for another day so I could sleep a bit and perhaps recover from the previous night's encampment in the John. I told them not to worry about cleaning the room since I just wanted to sleep and not be disturbed. When I hung up I put the Do Not Disturb sign on the door and slid into bed, got comfortable and began to doze off.

I was only a short time later when I awoke to a noise, opened my eyes and saw a maid standing there babbling something at me in Spanish.

I pointed to the door and told her, "Out!"

She held up towels and said something else as I kept pointing to the door, shaking my head 'no.' I guess she had no idea what that red hanging sign on the door was.

When she left I safety locked the door and threw over the bar that replaces the old chain latch. (No idea what that's called, maybe a 'non-chain lock' or 'safety bar that replaced the old chain lock') and called the hotel operator to tell housekeeping again to not clean the room until tomorrow, or until after I left at around four o' clock.

It still didn't work.

Over the next few hours I heard knocking on the door and people calling the room phone wanting to get in to clean. I just couldn't get anyone to understand, "Leave me the Hell alone!" I yelled.

Finally, I gave up. I showered, dressed, packed and checked out, telling them I would not pay for the extra time because no one would let me sleep.

My nap was at the airport before and during the flight to San Diego.

When I touched down at Lindbergh Field in San Diego I knew that once I got my bag and picked up the rental car it was only twenty minutes to the Hampton Inn and a restful night.

Turning off Grape Street onto the I-5 Freeway I could almost hear that soft bed calling to me. A few miles later I turned off the I-Five onto Fifty-Two and all traffic stopped due to a fatal accident about a mile ahead.

Since I was on the entrance ramp I was completely trapped, so I turned off the engine, closed my eyes and dozed off for a while until another emergency vehicle wailed its siren as it slowly squeezed along the ramp's shoulder.

Almost two hours later the traffic began to move and a few minutes later I finally turned onto Kearney Mesa Road and into the Hampton Inn's driveway a short time later. I was still weak and exhausted and could barely hoist my bags out of the trunk of the car so I dragged them along the edge of the trunk's edge until they dropped over the edge. They hit the ground hard because I didn't have the strength to bear their weight for more that a second or two. Extending the handles, I dragged the wheeled bags across the parking lot and into the lobby.

The cheerful girl at the desk smiled as I gave her my name for check-in. She efficiently brought up my reservation, ran my credit card but as she coded my key card, a God-awful noise blasted and echoed through the empty lobby. It was the fire alarm.

She retracted the key cards and told me the hotel would need to be evacuated and I would have to leave. So there I was, on my way back to the car, dragging my bags as I went. This time, I had to lift them into the trunk. They seemed to have gained about another thirty pounds.

As I started my rental car I could see people exiting the building and heard fire trucks on the way. I decided to leave all the commotion.

I drove along Clairemont Mesa Rd. until I spotted a supermarket. I figured I needed to get something into my stomach so I thought of Saltine crackers and Jell-O.

The supermarket turned out to be one of those big lot stores so I wound up with enough crackers to feed a few hundred parrots for a month and enough Jell-O to hold Jell-O-wrestling matches for the night, but I had my dinner.

I sat in the super market parking lot and munched a few crackers and washed them down by licking and sucking the Jell-O out of the cup. Since a spoon had not occurred to me at the time I bought the Jell-O and since I did not have access to a clamshell and a stick to improvise one, I reverted back to the way the cave men ate their Jell-O: the suck and slurp method.

Improvise: The code of a road warrior.

A half hour had elapsed so I thought that if the hotel was burned to the ground or water and smoke damaged I would have to go elsewhere, or if it was a false alarm, I should be able finally get into a room and feast on another cracker, or two and slurp some more Jell-O like a dog drinking from a tiny toilet bowl.

As I approached the hotel, the long, laddered, fire engine was rolling out of the driveway and the guests were reentering the building. It was a false alarm.

Finally, I could rest.

When I checked out of the Hampton two days later I hoped the maid was happy to get a free year's supply of Saltines and Jell-O.

***

Taipei's gastro-disaster was caused by the seafood buffet at the very posh and expensive hotel, the *Far Eastern Plaza*, at which I stayed. To give you an idea of the caliber of the hotel, former president Clinton was staying there at the same time I was. This was when he was on his book tour through Asian countries. What was his book title? *Chase the girls*? No, I don't think so—I can't remember.

There were of course many raw seafood items displayed and I guess one of them was from the last week's seafood buffet. This incident caused me some heavy-duty stomach discomfort for more than the usual one day. I did work the next day, but I started about five hours late and again looked like I was pulled from a train wreck.

Did you know there seems not to be any translation in Taiwan for diarrhea or vomiting? There is also no translation for any medication that stops diarrhea and there is no Pepto Bismol!

I *will* say that Frank, one of our engineering people in Taiwan, when trying to explain vomiting to him, he finally came up with the English word "pook." Close enough and he was able to get me something that was like an aspirin-sized Tums.

I chewed handfuls but it did little good.

I was still sick eight days after I returned back to the U.S. and had to take Cipro to knock it out. I now carry Cipro with me for the next time.

Once you have been sitting on the bathroom floor the entire night, wrapped in a blanket to quell the chills, drinking water just so you have something to throw up you will usually pack Pepto Bismol and Imodium for the rest of your travel life but not much seems to help the vomiting. No fear, we road warriors are a hearty bunch.

I also try to stay away from salad bars. It is not food anyway according to the overweight comedian, John Pinette. He says, "Salad's not food. Salad *comes* with the food."

***

If you get a cold or flu while traveling it is not difficult to find a store to get remedies to relieve your symptoms, at least in the U.S. However, having some standards such as aspirin gets you a little relief until you can get to a store.

Also, in the U.S. the yellow pages have many urgent care facilities where you don't need an appointment and will take a credit card. Some will even accept your insurance.

Another caution: many cold medications can make you drowsy, dizzy and some will dehydrate you.

Once I was seized by serious vertigo to the point that I could not stand up. It was from taking a prescribed cold medication. I felt like I was falling-down-drunk when I got up at four in the morning to catch a 7:30 flight out of Los Angeles. Unfortunately, I was driving to the airport.

Recovering a little, I made it to the airport, but just barely. This goes to show you the dedication or stupidity, or both in my career. I should have gone back to bed and missed my flight and rescheduled for a later one, but not me. I wanted to get home.

Below I have listed the things that I carry with me wherever I travel. I used to carry a travel iron and hair dryer, but most all hotels have them. The only hotel that I know of that usually does not have them is Red Roof Inn, but you can usually get one from the desk.

My traveling drug store contains the following:

Meds & stuff:

1. Imodium (very important when you need it, works good too)
2. Pepto Bismol tablets and Alka Seltzer
3. Zantac (helps stomach acid reflux caused by time zone differences of eating late then going to bed)
4. Aspirin or Tylenol (headache, fever)
5. Advil or equivalent (anti inflammatory for joints & aches)
6. Band-Aids
7. Antibiotic cream
8. Allergy meds, if needed
9. Preparation-H: Not necessarily for hemorrhoids. It can be used during allergy season for reducing swollen eyelids and keeps pollen from irritating the skin on your eyelids. The downside: It smells like fish-oil and makes everyone you see look like an asshole.
10. Saline nasal spray for dryness in airplanes and in some desert climates. It helps prevent nosebleeds due to dryness. Note:

if you have a serious problem with nasal dryness, there is an OTC product called Ayr Gel. It is a saline nasal gel that you can swab in your nose. It makes me sneeze a couple of times, but works very well and lasts much longer than a spray.

11. Lip balm for those dry regions such as Phoenix, Las Vegas and some parts of California, and when on a plane for an extended period of time.

12. Any vitamins or daily-prescribed medications, etc.

13. A digital thermometer (to verify you are really sick and may need a doctor)

Personal Care:

1. Of course hair items, dental care items, shaving items, etc.
2. Nail clippers & small nail file
3. Small plastic box with small bar of soap (in case there is no soap or if it is some garbage, smelly, hair laden soap in your hotel bathroom)
4. Sewing kit taken from one of the better hotel rooms you stay at. (If not already included, add a safety pin, or two—invaluable)
5. Shoeshine cloth taken from one of the better hotels. (Usually a small flannel cloth mitt)
6. Cologne or aftershave
7. Small nail brush (IMPORTANT ITEM) – Sure for nails or if you get grease or some other hard to remove grime on your skin, but it is also excellent to use with a few drops of shampoo and water to remove a greasy food stain from your shirt. Rinse the spot and use the hairdryer to dry it. (Great for all the clumsy, sloppy eaters— I know.)
8. If you are going to do a lot of handshaking at a large business venue you may want to consider some antibacterial hand lotion.

Optional items:

1. Spoon (for Ben & Jerry's, a yogurt cup or Jell-O)
2. A bottle of liquid shoe polish for emergency touch-ups (not

your hair, your shoes —well, hair is okay if you have the right color)
3. An eyeglass screwdriver (for eyeglass wearers)
4. And an old pair of glasses (in case you loose or break your current ones)
5. Small, pocket screwdriver for a slot head one side and Phillips on the other
6. Keychain flashlight or small Maglite™ flashlight. (In a pinch, your cell phone offers a little light)
7. An extra black belt (Once you forget to pack it, go buy one at your destination and leave it in your bag forever. Black goes with anything)

***

I just have to close this chapter with a food story.

At the time I was a sales manager and was traveling locally, in New Jersey, with one of my salesmen, Jim. We were calling on his customers during the morning and had no lunch appointment for the day.

Jim and I were getting hungry and we didn't know where any reasonably decent restaurants were located in the area. As we drove around I saw a Holiday Inn and told Jim they usually have a restaurant in those hotels.

We entered the nicely appointed restaurant and saw a sign that stated, "Lingerie Show Today." We looked at each other with that wordless expression saying, "Hmmm. That sounds pretty good."

We ordered sandwiches and the show began. Models were introduced and the brands of the clothes—well, almost clothes— were named along with where they could be purchased. Jim, with what is known as a 'shit eating grin' on his face said to me, "You sure do know the right places to eat, Bob."

As skimpy teddies and nighties paraded around the room Jim repeated the, "Man. You sure do know the right places to eat, Bob," comment a few more times.

Sandwiches finished, the waitress asked if we wanted coffee and desert.

"What do you have?" I asked.

She went through a list finishing with cherry pie. I nodded and said I'd have a piece with vanilla ice cream and coffee. Jim said, "Same."

The pie was placed in front of us and we began eating. After a few bites I started to notice the melting edges of the ice cream had developed a blackish color.

Jim was scoffing his pie and he didn't seem to notice the black coloring oozing from his piece. I began to prod my crust while mentioning to Jim what I was seeing in my plate. He stopped eating and started to probe his pie also.

I finally pushed my fork under the top crust of the pie and lifted it. To my dismay, there was a fine crop of hairy black mold growing proficiently on the surface of the cherry filling. Very disgusting.

Jim almost lost his lunch—literally. And I figured we would both wind up spending the night in the bathroom.

Jim swallowed hard and looked a little green and said, "Ya know, Bob, you sure do know the right places to eat."

The good news was we got our lunch for free, saw a lingerie show and didn't get sick.

Chapter 7

Interesting Flights

I have already told you about a few interesting, if not scary flights. I estimate I have been on about 1800 flights over the years and there have been only a few incidents worth mentioning.

In the early days with my cheap boss, we were to fly to Rochester, New York to visit some of our larger customers: Kodak, Stromberg-Carlson and Xerox.

We took our seats on the United Airlines 727 and buckled our seat belts. As we waited for the plane to depart the stewardess made the usual pre-flight announcement: "Welcome to United flight 134 to Orlando, Fort Lauderdale and Miami. We will be taking off shortly so please put your belongings in the overhead compartment or under the seat in front of you. Also . . ." The plane erupted in verbal chaos.

"What the hell happened to Rochester?" some guy shouted, getting up to get off the plane. Others were following.

After the red-faced stew checked with the pilot she picked up the mike again and said with an embarrassed chuckle, "Wait, folks. I forgot we're going to Rochester, New York first."

It is not reassuring when the crew is confused as to where they are going. But the stew was young, pretty and blond, so that explained it.

This was a rough flight because the weather was not very good and since it was a short flight, we did not get above twenty thousand feet. I noticed my boss was white knuckling, squeezing the armrests of his seat as the plane bumped as if it was running on a road full of boulders.

Looking 1970's dapper in my new three-piece suit; I received my breakfast tray from Miss Florida. Then, taking my first sip of orange juice, just as the plane hit another huge sky boulder, the juice spilled and created a nice contrasting color on my new duds.

Miss Florida took quick action with her trusty can of club soda. She shook the can into a cloth napkin to wet it. However, when the geyser of carbonated water shot me in the face I figured this was par for the blonds' course. Once she dried my face and blotted the juice stain she did save the day for me. It dried almost spotless— even my red face. A faint water stain was only noticeable to me.

Soon we began to descend, bumping and bouncing to the airport below. Mr. White Knuckles was getting whiter and it was getting bumpier until we finally touched down so hard I thought we may have been shot down.

The engines began screaming in reverse thrust and I noticed they were continuing longer than normal. Suddenly, the plane made an extreme, hard right turn, causing everyone to lean heavily to the left. I looked out my window in time to see the wing graze against a chain link fence at the end of the field causing a loud grinding noise that had some passengers screaming in panic. We had over-shot the runway.

The plane taxied across the grass and back onto the tarmac, then to the gate. Amazingly, not a word was spoken from the cockpit, or the stew crew. Miss Florida even smiled sheepishly and said the classic, "Ba bye," as we deplaned

Strike one, United.

***

I can recall six or seven aborted take-offs where we started racing down the runway and then suddenly, the pilot used reverse thrusters in hopes to stop before the end of the runway. Then the plane finally would hang a sharp turn just before hitting those banks of red lights. You were so close as the plane passed them that you could read, "OSRAM, Made in USA," imprinted on them as you went by.

These were no big incidents and after a short time, or an immediate second attempt, we were in the air. Just another pilot prank.

But to think, *"What if the rest of runway was too short by the time the decision to abort was made? Would we take off anyway and perhaps not be able to land safely—I mean crash? Or, would we punch through the fence, turn onto the freeway and drive all the way to Toronto?"*

These are some things that went through my mind at the time. But since I'm here to write this, it's a moot issue.

***

Perhaps this is a good time to make mention of some people's fear of flying. I just want state there is no need to fear flying. It is the safest means of transportation and you are more likely to fall in your bathtub, or be struck by lightning than to be in a plane crash. Truly, the noises, bumps and grinding sounds can upset the nervous flyer. However, do not fret. It is all explained simply and you will need to remember this for your next flights.

Grinding and thumping noises after take off are the landing gears retracting back into aircraft's body, *or* —perhaps one of the cargo doors is opening so hundreds of pieces of luggage will be strewn over a ten mile range. As the door tears off it may rip a large opening in the fuselage, sucking out several rows of seats.

The sudden silencing of the engines at some point usually means the plane has gained enough altitude in climbing and is high enough to put the engines in a slower cruising speed, or the plane may be entering its initial decent prior to landing, or— the plane may have run out of fuel and you will be plummeting to the ground very soon.

Whining noises heard mostly near the wing rows are the flaps being extended to get more lift as the plane reduces air speed when landing or retracting once fully airborne after takeoff, or— perhaps the wing may be loose and is beginning to tear off.

Some airports add to the noise scare tactics by observing special noise abatement procedures designed for that particular airport. John Wayne Airport, which is Santa Ana, California's Orange County Airport, is famous for special noise abatement procedures so the folks in the high rent districts such as Newport Beach and Laguna Beach are less disturbed by the jets taking off over their area. Usually the pilot will announce what will happen so not to terrorize the passengers after takeoff.

First the plane's engines will roar while the pilot has the breaks firmly locked and the engines cranking up. This is a little trick most of us guys did as a teenager if we had an automatic transmission in our car. We would sit at a traffic light, hold the break pedal down and step on the gas. When we would let the break go the car would burn rubber on the street signifying we had a really hot set of wheels. Yeah, testosterone! The same situation is here but without the screeching of tires and the pilot is not trying to impress anyone.

The plane then catapults down the runway and in a few seconds lifts off the ground with its nose up to the sky. I think this gets close to the feeling the space shuttle astronauts experience on blastoff.

After a short time of this pressed-to-your-seatback space launch, suddenly the engines seem to stop entirely and the plane feels like it will free-fall back to earth. But it doesn't. It just levels off and continues a normal climb to cruise altitude. First-timers will turn a little green on this one, so be advised if you are flying out of Orange County.

Two other airports that I have heard that pilots complain of safety issues are Reagan National, Washington, D.C. and LAX, Los Angeles International Airport.

Reagan National, I understand, has restrictions as to landing and take-off over the Capital and the White House and perhaps other important buildings. Because of this, pilots must navigate their aircraft to land or take off with wind directions not at optimum safety, usually over the Potomac River.

Similarly, LAX requires noise abatement procedures at night and forces pilots to fly over and past the airport and continue out over the Pacific. About halfway to Hawaii the plane will turn eastward and land with a westerly tailwind. This causes less lift and an earlier touch down on the runway and usually a longer and harder braking task so as not to over-shoot the end.

Aside from that the only other issue I can think of, which frightens some fliers, are high-altitude takeoffs in hot weather. I have had experiences in Denver, Albuquerque and Bozeman, Montana where I waited on the runway for hours until the temperature dropped. Obviously, there is thinner air at five to six thousand feet and less lift for takeoff. Hot and humid weather makes it even more difficult to get the plane off the ground before it runs out of runway.

Not to worry. They have the weight lift ratio down to a mathematical science, or at least a damned good guess, and they will not take off until the temperature drops a bit and it is deemed okay to take off. Just be a little patient for a few hours. It will take off eventually. Once you do, be advised you may start to think that your plane may be driving to your destination on the ground at high speed. It will take bit longer than usual to get off the ground.

Planes need to be spaced properly during landings and takeoffs. And why do you think that is? So they don't collide? Well, yes, but the primary reason is so the aircraft behind does not get into the jet wash of the one in front. And what is jet wash? It is the wake turbulence caused by the engines and wing tip vortices behind the aircraft. During take off and landings this is very dangerous because of the lower air speeds and angle of attack and at the lower altitudes there is less chance of recovery in this serious wake turbulence.

This happened to me once when landing in San Francisco. While looking out over San Francisco Bay on out final approach our pilot veered quickly off to the left and began a steep climb. I knew something was very wrong. He then announced that a foreign airliner cut in front of him unexpectedly and illegally which could have caused us to crash in the bay. He told us the dangerous pilot would be in deep trouble and the FAA would fine the airline heavily. The great response time of our pilot no doubt saved our lives—and his.

Clear air turbulence, or air boulders as I call them, is an invisible air demon that waits for your plane to come near and then it will try to knock the hell out of you. Nice bright sun, clear skies and you find yourself catching your drink in the cup as the liquid is coming back from the ceiling.

I always get a kick out of those people who suddenly experience the jolt from the turbulence and then look out the window to see what the plane has just tripped over.

Point here: Always keep your seatbelt on! This is why. Unless you have the urge to be peeled from the ceiling or have the air vent surgically removed from your skull because the plane dropped several hundred feet in a split second and your body didn't.

Turbulence can also be caused by stormy weather but since Doppler and other radar can usually determine these weather pockets, the pilot is usually re-routed around the worst of it.

My wife, who, most times needs to take Xanax or a gallon of Gallo in order to have the courage to set foot on an airplane sums it up perfectly. "I am not afraid of flying," she states. "I'm afraid of crashing."

The only reason she flies is so she can get to all of those great vacation spots and since I have talked her into coming with me on some business / pleasure trips she is getting much better. Especially when I'm in first class and she is in coach and I am not having claw marks in my arm.

I must admit that at one time, the closest I would sit near her was across the aisle. Yeah, yeah, shame on me, but I have justification. Even my youngest daughter won't sit next to her. She only behaves more calmly with strangers.

My flight time is usually to relax and catch a few winks of hibernation. If I am next to her when she is awake, I will feel fingernails sinking into my arm or her tapping me awake with a barrage of verbiage such as, "What's that noise?" or "I hate this," or with fear and almost teary eyes, "This is bad, isn't it?"

For people like this it does not seem to be any consolation by explaining to them that at any given time there are about fifty thousand people in the air and over the U.S. alone, and there can be as many as five thousand aircraft zipping from city to city at five hundred miles per hour, all without incident.

The fact that, "More people die on the road in one day than on planes in a year," also falls on deaf ears to people with this phobia.

One solution for these phobics is to issue them a parachute and tell them to put it on before take off so they will feel more secure but look stupid. It should also be explained to them as part of the safety briefing before take off, that in the event of a crash, they will be identified as the only ones who had just cause to be afraid and to all those who laughed at them and made fun of them for wearing a parachute, the last laugh will be on them.

How's that for satisfaction?

***

Continental Airlines became my first preference in carriers when they made Newark Airport a Continental hub. I could fly almost anywhere in the U.S. non-stop, which is a blessing, as it prevents you from having to change aircraft as often and perhaps have an additional delay or chance missing a connection.

So when I needed to go to Taiwan for the first time, I chose the big "C."

What I discovered was that Continental did not fly to Taiwan directly. They deferred to a partner carrier called Continental Micronesia for the Pacific link. No problem, or so I thought.

A travel agent arranged my schedule for this trip. To begin, I was to fly to Los Angeles and would spend a couple of days with my L.A. rep visiting customers. Then fly from L.A. to Honolulu. After a couple hours layover in Hawaii, the next leg was from Honolulu to Guam, an eight-hour flight. There was a twelve-hour layover in Guam so I arranged a hotel for a decent bed and a hot shower.

The next morning the flight was to make a stop in Saipan in the Marianas, then on to Seoul, South Korea, and from there, finally to Taipei, Taiwan.

Whew! Chalk up those miles.

I arrived in Honolulu on schedule and decided to go to the Presidents Club, Continental's club lounge, for some coffee and to call my wife. The line was busy as it was before I left Los Angeles.

My youngest daughter was thirteen and this was before the teen cell phone era. It was also before I succumbed to getting her own phone line and as you know, if there was a course in school for teenage girls called *Phone Conversations of Teenage Nonsense* most would rate as honor students in this subject.

My cup of coffee was finished and I closed my eyes for a few seconds and when I opened them, I realized I was the only one in the club. I had fallen asleep in the corner and the receptionist did not see me there to awake me for my flight. As I jumped up in a mild panic that I would miss my flight, she apologized for not waking me. Now I had less than fifteen minutes to run to the gate at the other end of the airport and board the plane.

As I got to the gate, sweaty and panting, I saw two other people standing there with a gate agent as the plane was pushed back from the gate. I looked at my watch and saw it was still about five minutes before departure time.

"Whoa. Wait a minute here. What's going on?" I said to the gate agent.

"Sorry sir, the plane has left the gate. You missed your flight," the agent said with a hint of sympathy in her voice.

"Not acceptable," I said, as the couple, stranded there as well, looked at me like I was going to be some sort of savior and the flight would come back to the gate. "That plane left early and I was checked in on it. You are supposed to do a seat count and page passengers for a last chance to board. Right? And not pull away early without checking. Right? When is the next flight?"

The agent knew I was right and the airline was to be responsible, because she informed me, and the couple, that the next flight to Guam was not until the same time tomorrow.

I stated, "Then we'll need meal vouchers and a hotel voucher."

She agreed and told us we all would be compensated with three meals and a hotel room for the night in Honolulu. It sure beats being stuck in Detroit by a long shot.

The three of us made the best of the problem. And since our luggage was on the plane, we took a taxi to a store where we could get a fresh set of clothes, then to dinner at a fantastic seafood restaurant. After some drinks at the hotel bar, a restful night followed.

The next day we met for breakfast then visited Waikiki Beach for a little sunshine until the early afternoon when we had to return to the airport. We did not want to miss another flight.

I still got a busy signal every time I called home. Very frustrating.

The flight to Guam was great because the three of us got bumped up to first class. The flight arrived on time, about 8:00 PM local time.

Guam is a jungle island and humid does not suffice as a correct description. Wet, disgusting and hard to breathe is more like it, and as I stepped out of the airport building I was not sure if I began to sweat or if I was collecting condensation. Either way, I was dripping wet.

.I now had my bag and I was ready for a taxi to the hotel and a quick snack. Then a shower and a good night's sleep, but it was too late to call home.

Before leaving the hotel the next morning I called home again and the phone line to was still busy, so I tried again at the airport even as the plane to Saipan was boarding. My daughter was the one to answer the phone and I dumped my frustration on her. I lambasted her for the overuse of the phone and told her to stay off of it so I could call occasionally. I then asked to speak to her mother. But my wife had just slipped out to the store for some milk. I was not happy.

It was only about an hour flight to Saipan. The plane was mostly Americans going to play golf and other resort duties on the beautiful little island.

We landed and exchanged American passengers for Koreans heading to Seoul.

Shortly after the plane took off from Saipan, the pilot did a, "Well folks," and continued with, "We have a little problem up here. It seems that our hydraulic system had a failure and we have almost no use of it. We need to land for the repair but Saipan does not have the proper emergency and fire equipment so we will need to return to Guam."

Hydraulic system, huh? I know this is not a good thing. The flaps, rudder, ailerons, spoilers, landing gears and the entire steering of the plane depended on hydraulics and fire equipment. Hmmm. Sounds serious all right.

I was in a first class seat and had been waiting to hit the lavatory while we were still on the ground before to take off. I figured I'd wait until we got up in the air and then go. So when the flight attendant asked me if I would help out with the emergency, I said, "Sure, but I have to hit the rest room first."

She replied. "I know. I feel the same way."

I skipped the explanation and just went to pee.

Since there were only about six Americans on the flight now and the rest were Koreans who spoke little or no English, the flight crew selected the Americans to help with the emergency landing procedures.

When I returned from the lavatory, the flight attendant moved me to the window seat in the right wing's emergency row and began to give me and the fellow on the aisle seat, Mike, a set instructions for the emergency landing.

After moving people from the seat in front of that row, she explained when the pilot calls out "Edward Victor," [EV for evacuate], I was to pull the release latch on the door, pull it out of its door jam and throw it over the seat in front of me. I was then to go out the door, go the edge of the wing's flap and slide down to the tarmac. Mike, the guy that was on the aisle seat, was instructed to help usher people out the door and onto the wing, and when they slid down the wing, I was to catch and assist them.

I looked around to see how many fatties might be pounding me into the tarmac. There were only a few.

She then said to me, "But if you see smoke or flames outside the window, don't open the door."

So as mister smart-ass, I asked, "So what if I see smoke or flames out both doors?" referring to the wing exit across the aisle.

She looked at me with a nervous expression and a forced, sick smile and just put her palms up and shrugged her shoulders. This was not good.

As we headed south toward Guam the pilot began to dump fuel from the wing tanks. Streams of vapor-like aviation jet fuel poured out the vents making the plane appear to be streaking toward disaster faster than it should.

During the next hour there were a lot of things that one can think about. You first consider you own mortality and wonder if you were a good person and if there really is a hereafter, will you be on the upper or lower levels. You begin to envision what it will be like to see that bright light at the end of the dark tunnel you have heard about and wonder if the light is perhaps coming from a huge freight train.

Then you begin to think about the good things in your life: your family, your close friends, and your pets. Will they really miss you? Were you worth it? The old, "your life flashing past you" thing.

We were flying over the Mariana Trench at 35,000 feet. The surface of the Pacific Ocean was almost seven miles below us; a long way to its whitecaps. The trench beneath its surface was 36,201 feet to the bottom, the deepest part of the ocean on the planet.

If this plane were to plummet into the water all of us on the flight would be fish food, and there would never be a trace of any of us to scoop up into a net or wash up any shore. Even the wussy ones with the parachutes on would not get their last, "I told you so."

I sat there at this point and filled with regret. Before getting on this flight I chastised my daughter and did not get to tell her, or my wife, I loved them. I hoped they would know that I did, if I didn't return home. Pondering all the things in my life that were not yet accomplished or not yet even pondered certainly put me in a mental rut.

The plane was silent except for the noise of the three jet engines but no one was sleeping or relaxed. Everyone just stared either out the window or just straight ahead. I assumed most were thinking similar thoughts to what I was thinking.

Then, my optimistic side took control. I figured the pilots didn't want to start a new career flying clouds and strumming a harp, so as long as they protected their asses, the rest of us were covered—unless they had already put it on autopilot and bailed out.

I wasn't long before the pilot spoke over the PA and told us that he was going to have to lower the landing gears manually, by gravity, and just as when the landing gear had a problem in Dallas, the flight engineer of this 727 was going to come into the passenger cabin and view the gears from a visual port under the floor panels to be sure they were down and locked. The pilots *were* still up front after all.

He also warned that when (if) we landed we had no nose wheel steering, which meant he had no steering at all once on the ground. This meant we would go where the plane took us and had no control.

We were cleared for landing and the airport was prepared for the emergency landing. Which meant everyone headed for cover.

The pilot made a pass at the runway but it was too wide to line up to center-runway so he throttled up and went around again. I hoped there was enough fuel to go around again, but not too much in case of a fire. Nerve-wracking. The second time around he lined up perfectly and began a straight descent to the runway over the mountain below. The weather was perfect and there were no strong winds so the glide path was unhampered. I looked out my window and saw water, then land ahead, then beneath us, now runway—here we go.

He touched down and smooth as silk, in fact probably the smoothest landing I can remember, and full throttled the engines in reverse thrust.

The plane veered from side to side, as the pilot used the engine's reverse thrusters, alternately throttling them, in an attempt to steer and keep the plane on the runway. This was working until the plane's speed dropped.

I looked out the window and saw a huge yellow fire vehicle with a large, chrome, gun-like foam-cannon, racing alongside the 727. I could see the men inside were wearing silver fire suits and headgear with goggles. They were ready for the worst. So was I.

The plane veered off the runway and began thumping over signs, lights and markers. Rolling on grass it began to slow down as it headed for some small buildings and fences several hundred yards away. With fire trucks flanking the aircraft, it finally rolled to a stop and sunk into the soft, grass-covered earth. There was no smoke or flames.

Surprisingly, "Edward Victor! Edward Victor!" Came over the PA, so I quickly unbuckled my seat belt, stood up and ripped the door from its frame. I then tossed it over the seat into the empty row as instructed, then climbed out onto the wing.

I quickly looked around again for smoke or flames, or any other reason why I should slide my ass down to the ground off that freaking high-off-the-ground wing and break my ankle, or entire leg, or legs, only to be crushed to death by fifty, or so, both fat and skinny Koreans as they piled on top of me after sliding off the wing.

I saw no immediate dangers. The fire vehicles were not doing anything but sitting in the location they stopped. But then, I saw the escape chute inflate out of the front right door and saw one Korean guy fly out the door screaming whatever the Korean word was for banzai, or shiiiiit!

Then nothing.

Mike, the aisle guy, then stuck his head out the door and yelled, "Bob! Bob! Don't go. They called off the E-Vac."

Great. If I slid down and broke bones it could have ruined my entire day. I'd be on the ground hobbling around trying to figure out what in hell the Korean guy from up front was trying to tell me. Probably something like, "Hey, Yankee boy. You asshole too for jumping out of safely landed airplane. We brothers now. We have reunion sometime." Damn right, cancel the E-Vac. No smoke or flames here. Let me back in the stinking piece of shit plane. "Sure, no problem, Mike. I'm coming in," I responded casually.

It took a while for the ground crew to get a truck with a stairway so we could vacate the plane—deplane, I mean. The Korean guy who bailed out helped the crew push the stairway to the plane in the soft grass and we all got out and walked to waiting busses.

No one had any idea how or when we were going to get out of Guam but I don't think anyone cared because none of us were currently sinking slowly into the deepest part of the ocean to sleep with the fishes. We were all alive and all uninjured and that was only because I elected not to break my ankle jumping off the damned wing and becoming the only casualty.

We were surely going to be grounded for some time so the Americans, including the flight crew, gathered together and decided to have dinner, so off the restaurant we went.

I congratulated and thanked the pilot and his crew for a job well done and was told, "We were just lucky."

Very reassuring.

The Captain lived in Florida. I thought that was a hell of a commute to work. But that's his road warrior story. Or, would it be air warrior?

After an enjoyable meal and some interesting conversation, information came that the part to repair the plane was on its way to Guam and was being flown in from the U.S. mainland. It would be another twelve to fourteen hours before it would arrive, then the repair would start.

Great. We were taking the same plane to Korea.

I finally was able to reach Mary on the phone and tell her where I was and what happened.

The next day I was in Seoul, then finally in Taipei only two days late.

Days later, a friend of mine called my home not knowing I was traveling. When Mary told him about the incident, he got all excited, telling her he saw it on CNN.

Apparently, there was a CNN cameraman, or someone who sent a video to CNN, showing the plane landing, swaying side to side on the runway, and then coming to a stop in the grass about fifty feet from a small building. I am sure they were hoping for a spectacular fiery crash video. Glad to have disappointed them.

What they did get was to video the lone idiot on the wing, with all viewers wondering what the hell he was doing there.

Hey, I'm a star.

Chapter 8

Hotels

Most national hotel chains are pretty good but some are better than others. Even within the chain itself some may be run poorly and others may be great.

What does a road warrior need most in a hotel room besides the usual amenities?

Answer: Electrical outlets.

With all the electronic gear we need to carry there are seldom enough outlets to plug in all the chargers. The rooms that are best have an outlet strip on or near the desk. Even still, I carry a three-way outlet adapter and use it most of the time.

Some rooms have all the outlets blocked by furniture and moving furniture is something I do not want to be doing after a long day. This something I could never figure out. It would appear the hotel management was too cheap to allow you the use of electricity to charge your cell phone.

Also, they will give you an iron but try finding a place to plug it in. Most times you will be setting up the ironing board in the nook outside the bathroom and use the sink outlet for your power source. This is usually somewhat cumbersome and difficult working in the narrow area but it is better than moving the bed.

The chain for which I have had the worst experiences is Ramada Inn. Oh, I'm sure some of you love the chain and have been lucky with a clean, well-maintained hotel. My experiences were all similar to the Saint Louis adventure: dirty, damp smelly, things in ill repair and ripe for a lawsuit.

One Ramada in North Carolina annoyed me because when I woke up in the morning, a maid was standing in my room and she startled the daylights out of me. After she left, I tried to get out of the bed and discovered both my legs went through different holes in the sheet and my tossing and turning during the night had me all knotted up and couldn't move.

Now that I think about it, maybe it was a trap set by that maid—some sort of maid prank, I guess. But since I'm not into bondage I was less than thrilled.

Another incident was in San Diego hotel, which is now gone, thankfully. The place was a dump with wet, smelly, stained carpeting and a dirty bathroom with someone's pubic hair still in the tub. Disgusting.

After a few strikes in a row I chalked them off my list. There is no use in adding stress in anticipation of a bad hotel room.

I of course have developed my regular favorites for the locations I visit frequently and they vary by location. Usually, if I select one of those favorites in a new location, the standards are much the same.

Holiday Inn and Hampton Inns are very consistent. Courtyard by Marriot is also consistent but because they are all the same; I actually don't like that. If I stay at a Courtyard in Phoenix today, then move to one in Indianapolis tomorrow, when I wake up I can't tell if I changed locations or not. It's just me. They're fine but I'm not crazy about them. So I guess I'm not into bondage *or* deja' vu.

Comfort Inn, Quality Inn, Sleep Inn, Clarions, The Choice Hotels Group, are all pretty good. Reasonable rates and usually well designed for the business traveler.

Recently I was very impressed by the Residence Inn Suites, also by Marriot—very nice for the rate.

The Westin, Hilton, and Radisson hotels are all good but a little more pricy, especially in the major cities.

Best Westerns are all over the lot. I stayed at one in Sunnyvale, California that was a disaster. It was difficult to find so I called the hotel, not knowing that I was pretty close, and still the clerk could not direct me to where he was.

After finding it two blocks ahead and checking in, the route to the elevator became another challenge. It was an obstacle course. There was no ramp so I had to lift my bags up a set of steps. Then, I had to cross a courtyard covered with a loose-laying outdoor carpet runner that kept bunching up under my wheeled bag causing it to stop. I had to back up, struggle with the runner until I finally got pissed-off and ripped the entire thing up and tossed it aside in anger and frustration. Then to add insult to injury, the elevator door kept trying to close on me before I could get in.

The room had been newly, but only partially painted and there was still a large unpainted area around the sloppy spackling job encircling the air conditioner in the wall. Not a huge issue. But the globs of crusty dried paint, lumps of spackling compound in the carpet, a large paint-spill area and footprints in paint were a little too much for the eye to accept.

Since the remodeling called for a new crown molding the old drapes had been lowered by about a foot and were lying across the floor to the extent that I would trip over them when I walked past.

As I mentioned before, we are a hardy bunch so the paint and the drapes were not going to interfere with my sleeping, so it was no serious problem.

It was 11:00 PM when I arrived at the hotel and since I had just flown up from L.A. to San Jose airport on a flight that was about four hours late. I was ready to crash land into the bed, which I did.

I must have fallen asleep instantly but a short while later my eyes popped open for some unknown reason. As I closed my eyes again I realized why I awoke. The bed smelled of body odor and it was not mine. How disgusting to discover you are in a skanky, smelly bed.

I got up and turned on the light, now noticing what looked like black track marks from someone's luggage wheels on the bottom sheet. Awful! The bed was never changed from the previous guest.

There was a musty spare blanket in the closet that didn't smell too bad so I wrapped myself in it and slept on the chair for the night.

No one seemed to give a damn at the front desk that morning when I complained and told the manager I was not paying for that night. I also wanted another room but was told they had none available. I was to have the same room, but they assured me it would be cleaned and the linens changed. Whoop-dee-doo—clean bedding!

When I returned later that day it was clean, accept for the paint, spackle and some heavy soap scum in the shower. The bedding was replaced and smelled fresh.

When I checked out the next morning there was a huge ten-dollar credit on my bill for the night in the chair. My comments and complaint fell on deaf ears at the front desk, so when I returned home I wrote a letter to the Best Western headquarters.

Best Westerns are mostly franchises: independently owned hotels. This can allow for the possibility for a poorly run facility such as Sunnyvale and the corporate office has little control over its franchisees. But as a traveler, once you get burned a couple of times you will stay away from any hotels in the chain, like I do with Ramada, and the well-run places suffer due to the stinkers.

With this in mind, headquarters sent me a courtesy voucher for fifty dollars. It was a good customer relations move and I used it in Huntsville, where that Best Western was as good as the best Hampton.

It pays to complain, if truly warranted. I was told that if a lot of people complain about a particular Best Western Hotel, eventually the franchise could be jeopardized. Somehow I seriously doubt it.

Personally, I never stay at mom and pop places of unknown name. Not to say they may not be fantastic, it is just that when you stay at most name brand hotels, you usually know what you are getting.

Recently, in Omaha I was forced to stay at an Econo Lodge because all the better hotels were sold out due to a huge college event in town. This was certainly not one of the finer hotels of the lesser category. However, the roach races in the evening were very entertaining. I won twelve bucks on Rodney Roach, Number 4, but then a rat ate him and I began to lose money on Crumb Eater, Number 12.

There was dried and not so dried coffee puddles on the chest of drawers where the TV sat, the hot water faucet in the sink did not work, the tub was moldy and when I awoke the next morning, I had two mysterious, swollen bites on my back.

You get what you pay for, but in this case the roach ranch was a hundred and forty bucks. I guess it was the entertainment cover charge.

One thing that most all hotels have in common is rough, scratchy towels. I'm not sure if this is meant to be an amenity so you can exfoliate some dead skin, and also several layers of live skin as well, or it is the industrial strength laundering they go through.

I could never understand people stealing towels from a hotel. Unless they wanted to use them to grind rust off their old pick-up truck, it is not worth going through the trouble, or pain.

One last thing: I could never figure out why in all hotels, good or bad, the terry cloth tub mats always stick to your feet when you step out of the shower and start drying off. It's a mystery to me. Maybe it's a tub prank?

***

Beware of in-room coffee pots.

While staying at a Howard Johnson's in Santa Clara, California I decided to make some coffee, using the in-room coffee maker. I took the glass pot, rinsed it out and filled it with water.

As I went to pour the water into the reservoir I noticed something was not quite right. As I peered into the receptacle, which I never had done before, I saw enough hairs inside to make a tiny toupee. Some were straight and some were more of a pubic construction.

Flecks of dandruff and a small fly rounded out the additional flavoring that would have been added to the caffeinated brew.

Since that time, if I am desperate for a cup of in-room coffee, I will inspect the entire appliance and still rinse it out thoroughly. However, usually I do not use in-room coffee pots any longer.

***

I have only ever stayed at one Motel Six.

It was clean and had some amenities such as towels and a tiny bar of soap—and I do mean tiny.

The towels were scaled down to where a washcloth was the hand towel and the hand towel was the bath towel. The only real problem was whatever fabric softener they used caused the towels not to be absorbent. So when I tried to dry myself, I just pushed the water around my skin. A squeegee would have worked better

Other then that it was . . . well, they left the light on anyway.

***

Are you afraid of the dark?

Me neither. But if you wake up in an unfamiliar room during the night you may do some damage to toes, shins or knees if you have your navigation settings wrong for your temporary location. Especially if you are in a different hotel room every night. You remember you got up last night and went to the right to the bathroom. But tonight, that might walk you smack into the coffee table.

Some rooms now have a dim red nightlight built into the hairdryer. However, my little suggestion is to leave the bathroom light on and leave the door open just a crack. It is just enough to get you safely to the John.

The downside of this routine is if the bathroom fan is not on a separate switch, and it sounds like a Blackhawk helicopter landing on the toilet when turned on, you'll need to turn on a bed light when you get up or keep a small flashlight at bedside. A two AA cell Maglite is my choice.

***

Personally I tend to stay at the same name brand hotels and I have my set ones in each area I frequent. When I find I am going to a new area, I still try to pick my preferred standards.

The most reliable choices for me are:

- Holiday Inn (Includes Express, Crown Plaza)
- Hiltons, Hampton Inn, Doubletree
- Quality Inn, Comfort Inn, Sleep Inn
- Residence Inn & Suites
- Red Roof Inn (But only if they have Executive King business rooms. Those rooms have an iron and hair dryer)

Bottom line is, make your own decisions by cost, location and amenities. If you choose wrong, let them know and don't go there next time. If it is good, use it again. If they get to know you may get a comp upgrade or some other benefit—like clean bed linens.

Chapter 9

Other Passengers

". . . So sit back, relax, and enjoy the flight."

Surely you have heard those famous starter instructions for your aerial venture each time you fly. They are simple, easy instructions after dealing with the hassles that finally got you to this point. Sometimes, however, it is not that easy to comply.

Most flights are uneventful and can be relaxing if you are able to read, watch the movie or sleep with some semblance of peace in your seat.

Unfortunately, it does not matter if you are in coach or first class, there are those whose charter it is to annoy you, in one way or another, for the entire flight.

***

Some people have no common sense or common courtesy. For example, board the aircraft ahead of most of the crowd and if you have an aisle seat, toward the front and just count how many times your get bumped, slammed and banged with side-slung shoulder bags.

Side-slingers are pretty bad but not the worst.

Also, note the "humpbacks." They are the idiots wearing backpacks, which will turn from side to side while shuffling down the aisle. Each time they turn their inconsiderate "hump" hits people in the head or face. These same people will quickly put the hump back on as soon as the plane lands and they then stand in the tightly packed aisle and rotate so to bang the hell out of anyone standing near by.

I have also experienced a number of humpback pedestrians in the Pacific Northwest who walk the crowded streets just to abruptly turn and catch an unsuspecting non-humpback off guard. And I love those humpy people in elevators. I don't get it. Why does one need to carry that much stuff around anyway? Worse, are the junior humpbacks, the kids who are wearing those huge backpacks, also known as "nutcrackers," if you know what I mean.

The airlines should make these stupid, inconsiderate people remove the hump while getting on planes. I suggested this once to a flight attendant and was told it would not be polite to do that. Sure. I guess it's polite to get slammed in the face.

Side-slingers and humpbacks should at the very least be told by the airline to carry their WFDs (Weapons of Facial Destruction) in front of them, not slung so aisle seated passengers need to dodge the bags as they pass.

Punishment for failure to remove the hump, or the shoulder-sling, should be that for every person they touch with the protrusion, that person gets to kick them two swift shots in their butt.

Do I sound bitter here?

Yeah. Sorry.

It happens to me all to often.

***

Some flight attendants are another source of annoyance. When they were in training my guess is they had a few less metric tons of butt to go swaying from side to side. Now, with the same consideration of the "humpbacks" they plow along, with their big bottoms careening from side to side, sometimes sending aisle-passengers reeling toward the windows.

To their credit, they seem to be trying to reduce their girth by vigorous exercise. That is, by stomping swiftly back and forth in the center aisle as they butt-bash most all they pass. Ultimately, no physical change in their bodies seems to occur. However, this is not limited to the wider crewmembers. I have experienced skinny flight attendants doing their fair share of inconsiderate butt-slamming as well.

Also, some flight attendants can't seem to drive the beverage carts without cracking elbows along the way. There have been a number of times when the warning to, "Watch your elbows," came a second or two after the pain.

The only solution for this problem is to suffer or don't get an aisle seat.

***

The next groups of annoyers are the ones who dally in the aisle and no on can pass them to get to their seats while boarding. This delays the boarding process and can cause the plane to miss its slot in the runway lineup for takeoff. If you see this happening near you, smack them in the back of the head then shove the person into their seat and quickly buckle them in. Be sure to step into the row when doing this so not to block the flow of passengers boarding.

***

A seat kicker is one of the worst annoyances and generally it is a hyper kid sitting behind you. God forbid, the parent tells him or her to sit still and stop kicking the seat of the person in front and behave like a civilized human. That would be considered child abuse to some or too much parental responsibility.

This scenario covers a larger scope of interruptions to your trip. If you are reading, it distracts you to the point where you read the same sentence over and over; if you are watching the movie, you start to lose the gist of the plot, or if you were sleeping—you won't be.

My best suggestion is to ask the parent nicely to tell the kid to stop. If that does not work, ask the flight attendant to tell the parent to tell the kid to stop. Last-ditch effort is to get out of your seat and bend down to the kid's level while in the aisle, then "evil eye" the little monster and tell him to stop or you will eat him alive.

***

Screaming kids and screaming babies are two different scenarios. The screaming older kid, four or older, falls into the same category as the kicking kid. By now the parents should have control over the brat's actions. If they don't, or just don't give a damn, you need to try the same tactic as with the kicker.

The screaming baby is uncontrollable. Usually the kid is experiencing ear pain because the parents did not give the kid a decongestant to try to keep the Eustachian tubes in his ears open so the air pressure, especially during take off and landing, does not cause pain in the middle ear. Babies can't chew gum or intentionally yawn to clear the ear pain so they scream. The kid's parents want quiet too, so you will need to just suck it up and use your noise cancelling headsets.

Warning: if you don't like kids, noisy or otherwise, never go to, or from, Orlando. The Mickey Mouse monsters will put you over the edge and you will deplane as a babbling idiot.

***

The seatback puncher is one that can cause serious problems on a flight—like perhaps—a fistfight.

This is usually a man who thinks he has more rights than you because he thinks he is better than you. You can usually spot this type because he will wearing a suit and an ugly tie and while still on the ground, he will be either talking loudly and importantly on his cell phone or incessantly playing with the e-mail on his Blackberry, or both.

Now, there is nothing wrong with ties, or even ugly ties. However, if you are dressing for business on a plane, you are probably a rookie who hasn't figured out that you should not try to make a meeting later in the same day—one of my previous mentions. However, if your goal is just to look impressive or important while on the plane, get to your destination and change into jeans and a T-shirt and go to Burger King for dinner, then you just may be an idiot.

Of course it is acceptable to get on the plane wearing a suit if you are done for the day and on the way home, or to another destination where you plan to spend the night. At least when you arrive in your rumpled, wrinkled suit you hopefully have a fresh one in your packed bag. If not, there usually is a steam iron in the hotel room.

You will quickly discover that as you sit in a coach seat with your arms folded across your chest so to not touch the person next to you, and if you are wearing a dress shirt, it will be terribly wrinkled in the chest and arms regions.

Regarding steam irons with suits; try not to actually iron it. Put it on a hanger and run the steaming iron across the wrinkles. You can also hang it in the bathroom and run a steamy shower, with or without you, and most wrinkles will flatten out.

I made the mistake of traveling in a business suit in the early years when Mr. Cheap-Ass wanted to keep that extra hotel day out of the expenses. I am a firm believer that learning things the hard way is sometimes best for the memory retention. I now find that comfortable jeans and a simple pullover shirt works well and look just fine for traveling and wrinkles are not and issue.

Back to the seat puncher. Once in the air, this type will take out the laptop or reams of paper and folders. He then begins to make faces of disgust because his coach environment does not afford him the additional space he thinks he deserves.

When the person in front of him reclines his or her seat, Mister Superbiz begins to get stressed and that is when he will punch or push the seatback in front of him.

Once, on a flight from San Diego to Newark, I had one of those guys behind me. Funny, I tagged him on the way into the plane and because I am a Platinum Elite member and also Million Miler with Continental's One Pass program. If I don't get upgraded to first class, I at least get to board right after first class. So I was in my seat when he boarded with the non-Elites.

He had all the attributes and actions of trying to look impressive.

My guess was he was on one of his first business flights and was trying to impress someone, maybe one of those sexy flight attendants. But having a bad haircut, ugly tie and a wrinkled, stained white shirt does not impress very many people.

During take off I was falling asleep and every time I did my head would nod forward, waking me up. Once we were at cruising altitude I elected to recline my seat just enough so I wouldn't look like I was bobbing for apples as I dozed off.

I had just gotten comfortable and began to doze when three jolts came rapping in the back of my seat followed by Mr. Superbiz stating authoritatively, "I'm trying to work back here."

"Really? And I'm trying to sleep up here," I replied casually and went back to sleep for a while.

A bit later I awoke to another series of bumps on the seatback and I figured it was time to hit the lavatory, but first with a stop at the seat behind me.

I got out of my aisle seat, turned around with my well-practiced Nicholson smile, leaned over and got right in the guy's face and said, "If you have a problem with not enough room, my friend, I suggest you buy a first class seat or take up the space problem with the airline."

Then for emphasis I feigned that I was starting to leave but then returned to within six inches of his face and said, in almost a whisper, "You know, someday you're going to do that to the wrong person, and *he* may have to leave the plane in handcuffs, but *you* may be leaving on a stretcher."

I then dropped the smile and applied my meanest eyebrow scowl and said softly, but firmly, "Don't hit my seat again! Understand!?"

I loved his expression and he was intimidated until the homely woman next to him, probably his wife looked at me and sneered, "Well, how much damn room do you need?" He then said, "Yeah," in timid confirmation to her question.

"I guess, all that I paid for, lady," and with that, I pushed my seat to its fullest recline position and that is where it would stay until we were landing. Then, I went to the lavatory.

Before I came back to my seat I mentioned the incident to one of the male flight attendants. He told me if the guy does it again that will be considered aggressive behavior and he will be arrested when we land. But Mr. Superbiz was really Mr. Superwimp and sat quietly for the rest of the flight.

The term "asshole" is more than acceptable here as well.

***

Then there is person in front of *you* that insists on having the seatback all the way reclined. So be it, the seat is meant to do that as I described earlier.

However, if you're in a coach seat, when a meal comes and with your tray table down you can't see or get at your tray, it is acceptable to nicely ask either the person or the flight attendant to ask if the seatback could be raised just during the meal. Usually it works. If not, trade seats with that kicking kid.

If you get someone who obviously does not fly often, you may need to tell him or her to put the seat up while on the ground so people can get into the row behind. Or, if a slipshod stew doesn't notice the seat is reclined during take off or landing, don't be afraid to speak up.

The reason for the seats to be up is for the safety of the row behind, for ease of exiting in an emergency and more importantly, in case the plane stops short while taxiing, your face will have more clearance before kissing the seatback as the inertia pushes you forward. I often wondered if the flight crew knows this because we are made to put the seat forward even when there is a bulkhead wall behind. I assume they were just trained to have all the seatbacks up and damned the reason why.

***

The incessant talker can be a blessing or a curse. To a nervous flyer it reduces the stress by taking the mind off the various noises the aircraft will make. But if you are a seasoned traveler you want to do your own thing. Hopefully, it is not incessant talking.

I always get a little nervous when a jolly retired couple rambles down the aisle looking at every seat number, both right and left, and finally take the window and center seat next to me. Then, Pa Kettle immediately introduces himself and Ma, as my "Seat Mates" and my new best friends, on the trans-continental, six-hour flight.

Instantly, Ma brings out a large carton of pictures of the grandchildren that they are on the way to visit. This can be serious but three things will work for this problem.

First try to feign sleep and hope they will leave you alone. If you are not tired this will be a problem. It is also a problem if they insist on continuing to talk to you even if you are tired.

Next, try putting on a noise-canceling headset (another required carry-on, by the way) or open your laptop to do something there. You know, the electronic high-tech devices may fend off the techno-tards.

If they still can't take the hint that you don't want to talk to them, step three is to just say to them loudly, "Shut the fuck up! I hate you!" . . . Nah, only kidding. Just say, "Excuse me, but I can't talk now I am [choose one] 'working,' 'sleeping,' 'watching,' 'listening,' 'meditating,' 'contemplating,' or best, 'imagining you two naked at a bus stop.'" That will usually handle the problem.

***

I always prefer an aisle seat. However, if the people next to you who may have a bladder problem disturb you, get a window seat instead. For me, I would rather be the disturb-ee than the disturb-or.

However, if you are a window person, beware of the moron who will not get up when you need to get out of the window seat. There are a few nuts that expect you to climb over them. If you are five-feet tall and ninety pounds, maybe—but us average big guys can't do it and shouldn't have to. Simply ask them to get up so you can get out. If they refuse and just pull back a little, step on their feet, stick your butt, or crotch, in their face and jostle them on your way past. When you come back, I'll bet they will get up and allow you access.

One warning about getting up out of your seat: Try not to grab the seat in front of you and pull yourself up. It is pretty annoying to the passenger in that seat. Use the arm rests to push yourself up and use them again when you return to your window seat.

Having said that, I thought it was very funny when on one long flight, an old woman got up frequently to go to the lavatory. Each time, she would reach too far over the seat in front of her and grab some poor guy's face and pull herself out of the seat.

I almost split a gut when one time she reached over the seat a little further and had her fingers up the guy's nose to the top of her finger nail, while straining and pulling to get up. He finally had had it with the poor old gal and politely, but firmly, told her to be more careful.

She wasn't careful the next time either. What a hoot.

I hope she washed her hands.

***

Sitting on the plane after boarding a flight in Chicago, I was pleased to see that there were no more passengers coming down the aisle. Pleased because the two seats to my left were vacant. That meant I could raise the armrest and stretch side to side and have some extra room.

Figuring the door was about to close, I buckled my seat belt, and then looked up the aisle and could not believe what I was seeing. Two of the largest people I ever saw on a plane were sidestepping and squeezing their way down the center aisle and could barely make it as their bellies and butts were pushing people over in their seats.

This couple should have taken one of those Ringling Brothers rail freight cars; I mean they had to have been a combined weight of a half-ton, or more and not suitable for a coach airline seat.

I just knew where they were going.

Sure enough, they stopped at my row and while panting profusely and dripping sweat, grunted and pointed to the two empty seats on my left. This had to be a gate agent prank.

When I stood up and moved into the aisle, Mr. Ringling reached into the row and raised both center armrests. Mrs. Ringling was the first to squeeze in. She put half of her huge ass onto the window seat, and sitting sideways with her back up against the window she eclipsed the window's sunlight.

When Mr. Ringling squeezed in, he slammed himself against the huge gelatinous woman who was covering the window and I saw that I had about twelve inches to get my not-so-tiny ass into.

Looking around, it appeared there were no other seats available. I would have welcomed a middle seat somewhere. But, no, there were none.

I asked him if he could squeeze in a little more (a little joke of my own) and he made a difficult effort to gain about another half inch for me.

By the time I wedged myself in, I was flat against his side and the aisle armrest was digging into my right side. It was sort of like the saying of being caught between a rock and—a five hundred pound sack of mushy hemorrhoid salve.

These two would have had a better trip if they had been made to buy three seats, or of course, two first class seats, or better still, a space in the cargo hold.

I arrived back home with a pain in my back from leaning out in the aisle at an odd angle while the armrest dug its way deep into my ribcage.

My position was also pissing off Bruce, the flitty flight attendant, because my body was leaning into the aisle and took pleasure in slamming the beverage cart into me during the beverage service.

He even had the nerve to tell me I needed to sit right and keep out of the aisle. I said to him, "You have got to be kidding me. I'll tell you what, pal, you sit here and I'll serve the drinks and knock the shit out of you every time I go past."

He said nothing more to me.

When the plane landed I popped out of that seat with a terrific pain in my back, and missing a small chip of skin on my arm which was left on the beverage cart, and my entire left side was soaked with sweat—and it was not mine.

I wrote a complaint letter to Continental and got a phony, politically correct letter back about *sensitivity*. It's funny how no one cares about the victim's sensitivity. After all I paid for a full seat and got only a partial one. I know Southwest Airlines would have made the Ringlings buy at least three seats or take the train.

Continental did give me a fifty-dollar shut-your-mouth certificate, which didn't cover the cost of the chiropractor's visits.

***

The Flatulent Freddie can be male or female and is difficult to deal with because you are not sure who it is. When a SBD (silent, but deadly) dose of methane reaches you and not only smells bad, but also may burn your eyes, there is not a lot you can do but close your eyes and hold your breath.

I usually fiddle around with the air vent, which lets the farter know you're on to him or her, unless the source is in front of you and they can't see that you are trying to blow the odor in another direction. However, other victims may think *you* are the source and you are just trying to disperse and dilute the brown cloud with the air vents. It's a lose, lose situation.

So aside from asking everyone around you to stand up while you play a CSI Seat Sniffer to determine the culprit, and then proceed to utilize the mallet and cork that you brought for the occasion, you will just have to breathe and bear it.

If *you* are the potential source, get up and go to the lavatory and spring the air leak there for God's sake, and take Beano next time

***

Cheese feet are worse than Flatulent Freddies. Those methane mongers are at least intermittent whereas cheese feet people are continuous for the entire flight.

Just a couple of weeks ago I was fortunate, or at least I thought it was fortunate, to be upgraded to first class.

The fellow next to me was a big, scruffy looking character: he was wearing dirty shorts, a T-shirt and dirty used-to-be-white socks and sneakers—a real first class guy. Looking at his sneakered feet I gauged them to be somewhere between size fourteen and Sasquatch.

As soon as the plane took off, his sneakers came off and up came the cloud of rotten cheese vapor. Then, round two, off came the sweaty, smelly socks so to expose both the inner and outer surfaces of the socks and the full outer aroma of the huge feet, to the surrounding air. Needless to say I was grossed out.

Since I was in seat 1A, which is a window seat with the bulkhead in front of me, this was a nice tight corner to hold the entrapped odor.

When lunch was served everything had an aftertaste of strong parmesan cheese. This is great for an Italian restaurant, but not for a shrimp appetizer, a turkey sandwich and a "fun size" candy bar.

It is my understanding that one time a flight attendant told Britney Spears to cover her stinking feet on a flight. However, no one told Chucky Cheesefeet to do so. Six hours later, my clothes smelled like a cheese factory in July and it took me quite a while to get the smell out of my nostrils.

One side note on this guy; he walked into the wet-floored lavatory with his bare feet. I guess that was the closest he got to washing them. I suppose that tells it all about Chuckie's personal hygiene.

***

Occasionally, you may get to sit next to some poor soul who has a severe allergy to bathwater and soap.

B.O. Billie, which can be a male or a female, can be as bad as Chucky Cheesefeet, only smelling more like rotten onions than cheese (Is all this talk of food making you hungry?). Unfortunately, there is not much you can do once the aircraft's door is closed except perhaps rub some strong eucalyptus salve under your nose.

So sit back, relax, and smell the roses—or whatever.

Chapter 10

Restaurants

When you travel to all the major cities you will have the opportunity to sample food from the finest culinary establishments in the world. However, some of you will be on limited budgets, because of cheapskate bosses like the one I had.

Until you are established and either on your own or fully supported by your company, you may need to keep to the TGI Friday's and Chili's price-class restaurants. There is nothing wrong with those types of restaurants; in fact, I like them. A high-end steak or seafood house or the best Italian restaurant in town needs to be an occasional reward for the aggravation you are subjected to during your travels. So take your best customer out to dinner or lunch on the company. The customer will appreciate it and you will get to spoil yourself for a while.

When you can't, check out the telephone book for restaurants. Then go on the Internet and search them out. The Internet will usually give reviews and list the price ranges and show the menus so you have an idea what you will be spending.

You can also ask around for advice. I don't recommend asking the hotel desk clerk because at the low wage he or she is being paid they most likely cannot afford eating out in great restaurants. So consequently, they have no first hand knowledge. However, some hotels have a list they can give to you of local recommendations that may be okay . . . or, perhaps not. Sometimes the restaurants may pay to be on the list. It doesn't necessarily mean they are any good.

Cab drivers are another bad source. Sure, they know where they have dropped people off, but that does not necessarily mean the place is good.

Ask your customers for suggestions because they have usually had some history of suckering in a few salesmen for a high-priced meal at some place where they would not want to pick up the tab.

It is best to ask for the specific food you want, such as Mexican or seafood, etc. Many times there are local "mom and pop" restaurants that are only known to locals and turn out to be fantastic.

As I mentioned previously, buffets and salad bars have been the sources of most of my food born illnesses. I usually try to stay clear of those.

Keep in mind that restaurant reviews are a subjective factor. For example, a person who usually frequents White Castle for lunch and loves those tiny little ground-up rats will probably think a burger at Ruby Tuesday's tastes like the thirty-dollar burger at Twenty-One Club in New York City. If you have eaten a burger at Twenty-One, Ruby Tuesday's will taste like White Castle.

It is all about quality of food, culinary expertise in preparation and presentation. But fat and greasy does taste good, too.

I have an associate that will buy some greasy take-out food and go to his hotel room to eat alone. If I have to eat by myself, I want some people around me so I can at least 'people-watch' during my meal. I spend enough time alone that hermitting myself in a hotel room and watching the food channel as I eat my KFC doesn't really appeal to me.

***

Once I had my rep in Indianapolis invite me to dinner— at my expense of course— to "the best restaurant in town" as he described it to me. He told me it was fairly new and the menu was "amazing" and the food was "out of this world."

I could hardly wait.

He picked me up at my hotel and drove for about twenty minutes. Finally, as we rounded a corner an elongated, stainless steel, railroad-car-style building came into view. The large neon sign in front flashed, *The Diner.*

"There it is," he said proudly.

"It's a diner," I said disappointedly.

"Yep, *The Diner*," he repeated, and didn't get the gist of my disappointment.

Growing up in the east, in the Newark, New Jersey area, close to New York City, I have eaten in diners extensively during my early years. They are open twenty-four-seven and you can get most anything from meatloaf to roast turkey to steak, eggs, ice cream, cake, five kinds of soup and anything you can think of any time of the day or night.

But it's *diner food.* With the exception of breakfast, because it is hard to screw up eggs and toast, that means most diners range from mediocre at best to awful, and it's always a crapshoot as to what you will get. The motto usually is, "If it's greasy—it's good."

Since this diner was a new experience to this person, and since his taste buds apparently were not honed to some of the better quality cuisine, this was the best thing since sliced kielbasa to him.

"Look at this! They even have juke boxes at each booth," he said, beaming at me.

"Wow," was all I could say. I felt like I had stepped into a time warp with this guy.

Obviously my rep was not accustomed to good food. He ate like he was starving and I wondered if he would finish by licking his plate. Happily, he didn't. *The Diner* was a prize to his pallet.

Great for him. But *The Diner* was, as diners go, on a scale of one to ten, about a minus four.

However, my rep still thought it was great.

I guess his wife's cooking *really* sucked.

***

Pizza is another one of those foods that has been ruined by area trends and non-Italian hands in the kitchen.

When Italians first immigrated to this country they came to New York. They did not enter the U.S. through Philadelphia, Chicago, Boston or Los Angeles—at least in the early days. They came through Ellis Island in good old New York City. The first thing they saw was the Statue of Liberty, not the Liberty Bell, not Paul Revere's house, not even the place where Mrs. Murphy's cow caused the Chicago fire and leastwise, watching surfers as they entered the Port of Los Angeles or San Diego.

What's my point, you ask? The New York City region still has the best pizza and Italian food. Sure, sure, you say I'm prejudiced. Maybe. And sure, sure, you say – Boston, Philly and others have Italian neighborhoods and have some great restaurants. True, but for total numbers of great Italian food emporiums, New York and New Jersey top the country. If I do a search for Italian restaurants in a twenty-mile radius from my home in suburban, Northwest New Jersey, I will locate one hundred forty-eight Italian restaurants. Some are pizza places that also serve some of mama's finest cooking. If I do the same search from lower Manhattan I'll get over fourteen hundred Italian restaurants

Not to dispute that Italians have relocated to Philadelphia, Boston and Chicago and still make great pizza, but as to the number of small, independent mom and pop restaurants producing the best Italian food outside of Italy, the New York / Northern New Jersey area has the others beat by a mile.

Pizza is made from basic ingredients: pizza dough, tomato sauce seasoned with oregano, and other spices, olive oil, mozzarella cheese and a selection of *Italian* toppings, such as pepperoni, sausage, anchovies, onions, peppers, extra garlic or all of the above. The water that is added to make the pizza dough is a key factor in the quality and flavor of the pizza's crust. Therefore, if the local water used in the dough-making has high chlorine or very heavy minerals, or even too little minerals, it can make a lesser quality dough.

California is another story. I am amazed at the bastardization of pizza that has been created there. Ham, turkey, pineapple, strawberry, Spam, M&Ms, chocolate, cauliflower & broccoli or peanut butter and jelly are not in the original recipe. I'm sorry, but that is not pizza. To me, that's dumpster food.

Once in California, while traveling with my wife and my youngest daughter who was fourteen at the time, we stopped for lunch at what appeared to be a nice, casual outdoor restaurant in Orange County. My daughter ordered a slice of pizza and was asked by the waitress. "So like, what do you want on it?"

"Just plain," she answered.

The waitress looked dumbfounded. "Plain? Like, you mean, like, just the crust?"

Now it was daughter's turn to look dumbfounded so I stepped into the conversation. "She wants cheese and tomato sauce. No other toppings," I told Miss Menses.

What I wanted to say was, "Like dude-ett, it's like not a like freaking like pizza without like cheese and like tomato sauce, like, you idiot." But you can't fault a person for their ignorance to real Italian pizza, New York or New Jersey style or the over-abundance of the use of the word 'like'. If that's all they know, it's normal to them.

Regarding "normal:" Once, in California, I asked a customer to join me for dinner and asked him what kind of food he liked. "Italian," he told me.

"Let's go to the best place in town," I said.

"Fine," he replied. "Meet me here after work."

I met him at his office parking lot at 5:30 that day and he told me to follow him since his home was close to the restaurant and he would not have to come back to the office for his car.

I followed him for a few miles and finally he turned into the restaurant's parking lot. It was an Olive Garden.

Sadly, Olive Garden was the best Italian restaurant in the area.

You may be thinking, *Yeah, so what's wrong with Olive Garden?*

Nothing is wrong with it, but if you think it is the best in town, obviously you have never eaten at a real Italian restaurant. When you do you will surely taste the difference.

The chain pizza places are ones that I avoid. I recall once ordering one of those pizzas because I was trapped in my hotel without a car and no restaurants within walking distance. You know the one. It's the pizza chain where the kids who deliver it drive like a madman to get it to you before it gets and has the worst record for safe driving. The one where if you stood all their pizza boxes on end and placed them face to face, then pushed the first one down, they all would fall like. . . .

After a few bites I decided to eat the box instead. It tasted less like cardboard than the pizza.

***

A good suggestion is to keep a database of restaurants. If you are good at Microsoft Access databases, set up one for restaurants. I created one that sorts by airport code-letters, then by type of food.

I have a rating system from one to ten for food quality and notes about service. Sometimes the food is good but the service is so poor that you would not want to go back again. You can also make a note of the name of a superior waiter or waitress you may want to request the next time you are there.

***

Some years ago I stayed at a motel in Georgia and when I was to be seated for breakfast in their restaurant, I was asked if I wanted to sit at "the business man's table."

"What's a business man's table?" I asked and was told it was a large table where ten people could sit, chat and make new friends. Of course this politically incorrect title was many years ago when there were almost no "business women" who traveled.

This was a great idea. Since most of the time we road warriors sit alone it is nice to have a little conversation with others in the same business mode as you. I wish it caught on but that was the only time I ran into it.

In short, restaurants are subjective and everyone's personal taste is different. I can assure you, once you are on the road for a while you will begin to cultivate your taste buds and will become very judgmental of the food you eat and the service the establishment provides.

Chapter 11

Rental Cars

Rental car companies are all pretty much about the same but you will steer toward the ones who have the most convenient locations and with "on airport" locations being preferable. Although, the current trend is for airports to build "Rental Car Centers" off-airport for most all of the rental car companies.

There are only a few simple precautions to take with regard to rental cars. As you may recall, one of my previous comments how you will be charged for damage if you didn't notice it when you picked up the vehicle. So do a walk-around and be sure any damage is duly noted in writing before leaving the garage or lot and don't lose your copy. Also, keep it afterward for a while so when you get a letter about the damage, send a copy of the damage statement. Better idea still—don't take the car. Get a different one.

Another useful tip is to memorize at least the last three numbers or letters of the license plate. Why? Because it is not your car and a lot of cars, especially rental cars, look alike.

For example, while in Dallas once I stopped at a convenience store for some mints. I parked my blue Chevy rental at the side of the building. Mints in hand, I returned to the car and got in. As I put my key in the ignition I realized the key was not going to turn. I also noticed that the papers I left on the passenger seat were not mine. Whoops, wrong car. My blue Chevy was two cars away. Just as I was getting out of the car the guy to whom it belonged was coming out of the store. He looked at me with a "what the hell are you doing in my car" expression.

People in Texas can legally carry guns so I quickly apologized and explained my rental car was to the right and I mistakenly got in the wrong car.

He chuckled and told me his was a rental also and originally was headed for my car but realized it was not the correct plate number.

So from then on, I noted the plate number. A plate number would also have helped me the time I rented a white Ford in Miami.

My flight got in late, around 2:00 AM, due to a delayed inbound flight, and I had a very early morning meeting. I was tired and cranky and not only did I not note the plate number; I never even noted the model of the car. When I got to my hotel I went straight to bed.

The next the morning, I only remembered my rental vehicle was a white Ford. I also stuck the rental agreement in the glove box so from outside the vehicle there was no way to tell it was a rental. At 7:00 AM I was in the hotel parking lot looking at four white Fords all parked in a close proximity of each other. Which was mine?

There was no remote entry or plate number on my key ring so I went to the one, which was my best guess. Looking inside I saw nothing to identify the car as someone else's, but nothing to identify it as mine, either. My contract was in this vehicle but was hidden away in the damned glove box where I put it last night. Unfortunately, the key did not work in the door so I moved on to the next white Ford.

Did I leave any folders on the seat? I couldn't remember, but there were none in this car anyway. I tried the lock and nothing, so on to the next.

The third car had a maroon interior and I was sure the car I rented had dark gray, but I tried the key anyway. Nothing.

"Who gits the medium rare," came to mind. A no-brainer now. I knew at that point which was the correct car. I should have started at that end first.

What the hell . . . ? The key didn't work in that car either, but I was certain it had to be one of the four.

I went back to the first car and tried again. Still no luck, so I went down the row and tried again. Nada!

At the last vehicle I decided to try the key in the passenger door—nothing.

I tried the passenger door of the next cars then moved on to the car I had tried first. Its passenger door opened. The lock was broken in the driver's door. Murphy's Law in action. Had I known the correct car by the plate number I would not have wasted all that time.

Okay, so if you still think you will just need to know the color of the car, be very careful.

Once I picked up a car in San Jose at the outdoor lot at night. I took what looked like a dark purple Pontiac Grand Am but because of the yellow glare of the sodium lights in the lot I assumed the car was probably gray.

Surprise! The next morning, unbelievingly, matching the memorized plate number, I discovered the car was bright red. Red! I was shocked and didn't believe it at first. The plate matched and the key worked so it was the right car.

***

Some other things to watch out for are mileage charges. Most companies will give you unlimited miles unless you rent a large SUV or specialty vehicle such as a Hummer or a sports car.

Alamo used to be my first choice until, unknown to me, they modified their policy where if you dropped the car off at a location other than from where you picked it up, you were charged a mileage fee for your entire trip.

Many west coast trips scheduled me to fly into, say, L.A., and return home from San Diego, or maybe I would fly up from L.A. to San Jose and return the car to fly home from San Francisco. When the policy changed, unknown to me, I got nailed for a couple hundred dollars for mileage. That was the last time I used Alamo. They may have changed that policy but I really don't care. I am happy with National or Hertz. Besides, the same company now owns Alamo, National and Enterprise. Funny how once I have a bad experience and I change my venue, there is no need to go back until some serious dissatisfaction occurs with the new venue. Even then, one tends to go elsewhere and not back to the first company. That is why customer service is so critical.

Alamo was beginning to decline on my popularity list shortly before the mileage issue because of poorly maintained cars and declining customer service, which I'll tell you a story about next. Because of the rental in San Jose and the rip-off drop fee at San Francisco, I bagged Alamo for good. I guess I'm a tough customer.

***

Another time, an associate and I were to work a trade show booth with one of our distributors at McCormick Place Convention Center in Chicago.

Thinking we would be taking a group of people to dinner I thought it best to reserve a Cadillac so we could fit six people comfortably in the car.

After landing at O'Hare, then picking up the car from Alamo, then heading for downtown, I realized I had taken a wrong turn somewhere and knew my associate and I were off course. Using a need for gum as an excuse, I stopped at a convenience store to also ask for directions to get to downtown.

When I came out of the store, the car door was locked but my associate opened the locks when I tapped on the window.

"Why did you lock it?" I asked.

"I didn't," he answered. "At least I don't think I hit the button."

I disregarded it and continued on to Chicago.

That evening it was decided we would take four of the distributor people to dinner at Morton's Steakhouse. Since we were all staying at the same hotel we met in the lobby and got the car from the valet service. Because Morton's is in the heart of downtown, there is no parking lot or available street parking, so to a parking garage I went.

I drove into the garage, stopped and we all got out. A huge, ugly, mean looking guy who could have been the guy who played Lurch on the *Adams Family*, handed me a receipt and we all headed for the restaurant.

As I got within a few feet from the exit, Lurch bellowed, "Hey! Hey you! The door is locked."

Knowing the keys were inside and the windows shut, my stomach began to tighten. I told the group to go ahead; I'd catch up with them in a bit.

"You're blocking my business here, Buddy. You got a spare key?" he asked, glowering at me.

"No. It's a rental. The door locked by itself earlier today. I'll call Alamo," I replied.

Still in the early days of cell phones, I was 'cutting edge' with my Motorola flip phone. But back then, the term *roaming* meant when you left your home area, and I mean your actual town. Then, the roaming charges were a dollar per minute.

I called information for the number and then called the Alamo location at O'Hare.

When a girl answered I explained I was locked out and blocking the entrance of a downtown parking garage and I needed someone to come with a key, a crowbar or a hand grenade and get the car out of the way before Lurch killed me. She just said, "Hold on."

A few minutes passed and a line began ringing. Then the line was picked up by voice mail. "Hello, this is Dan. I'm away from my desk so leave your number and I'll call you back," it said.

There goes five bucks for nothing.

I didn't leave a message, but hung up and redialed. The same girl answered, "Alamo"

"Listen," I said. "I just called about blocking this parking garage and you put me through to Dan and I got his voice . . ."

"Hold on," she said, cutting me off and put me on hold again. And hold I did, until finally I hung up and called back.

"You just put me on hold and forgot about me. Don't you understand I need to speak with someone? Now!"

"Hold on"

"Hello, this is Dan. I'm away from my desk so leave . . . "

I hung up and called back again. I was fuming. "Do not! I repeat do not put me on hold again! Do not give me to Dan's voice mail! Get me someone on the line immediately or I will have your Cadillac towed and dumped into the Chicago River. Do you understand me?" I shouted at her.

"Hold on," and she put me on hold before I could say anything more.

Finally, "Hi, this is Dan. How can I help you?"

After explaining everything again and now up to about thirty dollars in roaming fees, Dan said, "No problem. Hold on," and disappeared for a few dollars/minutes.

Back on the line, he said, "Okay. Here you go. Call 1- 800- 623 . . . "

"Wait a minute," I said. What the hell is this number?"

"Oh, it's for Cadillac roadside service."

I was standing there, no pen or paper in hand and this jerk is telling me I have to call Cadillac roadside service. "Listen Dan, can't you call them for me?"

"Nope. Sorry, I can't," he said.

"Dan. This is not my car and I rented it from Alamo. *You* should call Cadillac for me or get someone else here to unlock it."

He repeated, "Nope. Sorry, I can't."

The Asshole!

It was my turn to tell him, "Great customer service here. Hold on," as I asked the big looming monster for something to write with and on.

I hung up on Dan without a thank you and called Cadillac. The line was answered by the typical, "Your call is important to us (but not important enough to answer) so please be patient and it will be answered by the next available agent."

Ca-ching, went the roaming meter for the next twenty minutes while I listened to elevator-type music. Finally someone came on the line and I blasted the poor guy.

He told me to calm down, give him the address and someone would be there as soon as possible. He then told me to just leave the car and catch up with my friends and go to dinner. I told him they were probably finished with dinner but maybe I could at least get dessert and a sandwich "to go" since an hour had passed.

Lurch's frown went only horizontal when I handed him two twenty-dollar bills for his inconvenience and walked to the restaurant. I guess he was elated.

They all were a little tipsy from drinking at the bar while waiting for me. But they were now already seated and had finished their appetizers. So I just ordered my entrée and we were back on track.

When we returned to the parking garage I had chalked up about a hundred dollars in roaming fees, forty bucks to the Adams family butler to ease the fear for my bodily well being, and not to mention the expensive tab at Morton's. But I was thankful the car was no longer in the entranceway of the garage. When we got to the garage kiosk Lurch was no longer there. I assumed he went to spend his forty dollars on some vice.

I didn't miss seeing him again.

Recently, I had a rented Infinity M35 with the same auto door locking issue but since Chicago, I have learned to always open the driver's side window if I am leaving the keys in the ignition. It can save you a huge bit of aggravation.

***

While on a trip to Los Angeles with the same bad-luck charm from the old days in Pittsburgh, John and I decided we would take a day out of the sales call schedule and go to Comdex in Las Vegas for one day. We would help out at the booth of some friends and get to walk around the show as well.

Comdex was a computer show that drew more than a hundred thousand computer nerds from around the world. There was a saying about most of these attendees and that was, "Comdex attendees bring only two things with them to Las Vegas: a pair of underwear and a hundred dollar bill—and they don't change either."

Because most of them did not gamble, the hotel room rates were doubled or tripled and some had a minimum four-night stay requirement. However, I was lucky and got two rooms for one night at some dump on Boulder Highway, on the outskirts of town.

Since we were only going to be gone for one night I decided not to turn in the National rental car in L.A. because we would be back the next day. We parked at LAX and flew to Vegas.

I had arranged another National rental in Vegas and when we got it I drove directly to the convention center, parked, and went to the booth that we were to meet our friends from Taiwan and assist them with their booth duty.

When the show closed at six o' clock we went to the parking lot and drove off to find the fleabag hotel I had arranged.

Fremont Street is in old downtown Las Vegas. It also becomes Boulder Highway as it veers to the southeast and goes toward Henderson. From the Strip I turned right on Fremont Street and drove slowly, trying to find the hotel, without success.

I had the address and phone number in my bag, which was in the trunk, so I pulled off into an open area which I thought was an abandoned gas station, or at least it appeared it had been closed for quite some time. Judging by the graffiti and the broken glass, I assumed this was not a great area, so before I got out of the car, I looked around first.

There were a few hookers on patrol across the street and a couple of derelicts wandering around about a block away. I got out, opened the trunk, got the paper with the hotel's information on it, and got back into the car to call the hotel for directions.

The person at the hotel told me I had gone a few blocks past their facility. I needed to turn around, turn up a small side street, and then I would see the hotel. No problem, I thought.

I took the key out my pocket and tried to turn on the ignition.

It would not turn.

This is not an uncommon problem. Occasionally, you need to be sure the shift lever is all the way in the Park position and sometimes, if the car rolls a bit while shifting into park, it can engage the ignition safety switch. That's no big deal.

With all the wiggling of the key, jiggling of the shift lever and even pushing and rocking the car, the key still would not turn. Here we were, now with memories of Pittsburgh creeping into my mind while derelicts and hookers were walking by with curiosity. They may have thought we were DEA or vice cops in an unmarked car because they didn't approach too closely.

We had made arrangements to meet our friends for dinner and now it looked we were going to be late.

I called National and did not have a problem getting someone to help. I guess I was sounding very annoyed and disappointed with the car so they said they would send someone as soon as they could.

"Sooner," I told them.

We waited about forty-five minutes and during that time I had called twice to tell them to get moving, we had an appointment to keep. I wasn't in the most pleasant of moods so I guess I was pretty nasty to the poor guy who was trying to help me.

Finally, a tow truck, which had the same model Buick Century hooked to it, was turning into the old gas station where we were stranded. I looked at John and told him this was all his fault. He is the unlucky talisman I had with me again.

The first thing the tow truck drivers asked was, "Did you try rocking it? Or, jiggling the key or the shift lever?"

We assured him we did but he had to test it on his own so to believe us. When he got the same results as we did, he dropped the towed vehicle for us, gave me the new keys and took the defective ones to include with the car he would tow back to the lot.

We had been unable to raise our friends on the phone so at this late time, we decided to forget about checking into the hotel and go right to dinner and meet them at a restaurant at the Rio. After dinner we got back in our new Buick Century and finally found the Hotel Fleabag, parked in front of it and went inside to check in. It was almost midnight.

Our rooms were upstairs, in the rear of the two-story structure, so we got back into the car to drive around to the other side of the building. Again, the key would not turn. Now I started to hum the tune *Welcome to the Hotel California*.

I was baffled and pissed off. I had rented the Buick Century model before and never had this problem. John suggested there might be some sort of a key release, or locking, mechanism. I could not find anything so I looked in the glove box and luckily there was the car's manual.

"Let's just go to our rooms. I'll bring the manual and if I can't find anything I'll call National again," I said.

We then got out luggage and ventured around to the rear of the building and up the stairs, struggling with our bags to our rooms.

Sitting on the bed, looking through the manual for some secret latch for the key I became more frustrated and tossed the book down and dialed National again. This time I spoke to a woman and was being short with her because I was aggravated about the 'key' business and it was getting pretty late. Recapping the evening and the events prior, I then asked, "Have you had this problem before with the Buick Century?"

"No. Not that I'm aware of," she replied.

Sensing I was getting really annoyed with National she told me she would have another car sent over to where I was. "But I'll need the plate number of the vehicle, "she said.

"It's after midnight and I want to get to sleep. I don't want to hang around waiting for your driver to show up and I certainly don't want to go outside, walk all the way to where the car is and get the plate number," I stated with an attitude.

She told me not to worry. The plate number was on the key ring. Just give it to her from there.

"Oh, okay," I relented, and reached into my pocket and pulled out the keys.

I read the number and she hesitated for a few moments and then said cautiously, "No. That's the plate number for the car we picked up from you earlier."

Oh, oh. A bell went off in my thick head and I again reached into my pocket and amazingly, found another set of National keys. When I gave her the plate number on those she said, "Yes. That's for the car you have now."

It was all coming together. When I dropped the key into my pocket after opening the trunk in Derelictville, I reached back into the pocket, not realizing I had pulled out the keys from the Buick Century that was parked at LAX. That meant, National had those keys and I would need them when I got back to L.A. tomorrow.

This had been the best odds in Vegas. For the entire day my odds were fifty – fifty that I would grab the wrong or right key. I had two winners: at the convention center and after dinner. And two losers: at Derelictville and now at the hotel.

So was I even? Not hardly.

I took a huge bite of humble pie and told her what happened. Then asked, "Where are the keys from the car you towed?"

She told me to hold on and a few minutes later, the same guy I was being impatient with earlier, came on the line. He was laughing.

"So how can I get the keys?" I questioned.

I sensed the satisfaction in his tone. "First, my friend, there will be the matter of a one hundred fifty dollar towing fee. "Should I just add that to your credit card?" he asked. I knew he was also thinking, *Did you want fries with that towing fee, asshole.*

I could just see him smiling. "Sure. No problem."

"Be here tomorrow between seven thirty and eight and ask for Tommy. He'll have the keys."

No fries? How about a glass of milk with that humble pie, sir?

Chapter 12

Baggage

Luggage is a very important piece of gear for the road warrior. It has to be versatile, durable and as lightweight as possible. It should be able to be over packed, over used and under appreciated. Yes, it should be able to be taken for granted.

Zippers should look like large meshed tank-treads and able to smoothly close and securely seal the heaviest of ballistic nylon compartments.

Yes, I said Nylon. Leather is beautiful when it is brand-spanking new but it will look like an old saddle from the Civil War after a few flights.

Your bag does not have to look good, nor does it need a designer name or label. Most of those bags are actually poor quality knock-offs and are made in China with no legal relationship to the designer at all.

The best rule of thumb is to buy the best bag you can; spend the five-to-eight hundred dollars and you will save money and have fewer problems in the long run.

Did you ever watch baggage handlers at the airport? Watching them load bags into the plane they look like frustrated professional wrestler want-a-be's. They body slam every bag they place on the conveyer with apparent malice, then the next handler will fling it, or toss it onto the plane's belly or into the baggage truck if it just landed. It is as if those fellows hate their jobs and all those poor bags are going to pay the price.

Two to three hundred dollar bags can't hold up for very long with that rough handling. And your new, sexy, expensive, but cheaply made designer bag will look not-so-sexy after a few trips. One day you may see your tighty-whities coming off the conveyer one at a time onto the baggage carrousel. Just hope they are clean.

It is embarrassing when the baggage is taking a long time to come up because it is your bag that is jammed in the conveyer. Then, after some of your clothes come up, your bag flops out with the zipper broken, your shoulder strap is gone and half your clothes are missing. The side has a large tear in it and the good news is that you still have one shoe left and it is hanging out the hole.

If you're lucky, you can fold and jam the shredded heap into a bundle and gather it into your arms and hug it all the way to your rental car. This really sucks! Believe me, I know. I've been there. It happened as described in Atlanta during my early days. My last cheap bag.

In my opinion, some of the best bags on the market are Andiamo, Tumi and Hartman.

Tumi makes a lower end bag under another brand name, Dakota, which still stands up fairly well. An associate of mine has one and has used it for a while with no problems.

My wife has Hartman luggage and finds it very serviceable. I also have a Hartman briefcase that I purchased in the '70s; I used it for more than twenty years. It is now retired but still in great condition, sitting in my office collecting dust because I don't have the heart to get rid of it.

Personally, I have used Andiamo luggage for more than twenty years and see no reason to get anything else. My first Andiamo bag was used for over three hundred flights and the only reason I retired it was to replace it with another Andiamo bag, but with wheels.

That is still my current bag and it has over five hundred flights under its buckle and will probably stand up to several hundred more before I may have to retire it—or myself. Another benefit of buying a good bag is that if there is ever a problem, defect or damage, the companies I mentioned will repair or replace the bag quickly and efficiently, usually with no or little charge.

Two additional tips I recommend: First, buy a colored luggage strap and tie it around your bag after you are packed. It will reinforce the latching mechanism of a fold-over garment bag and also a latched hard bag or even zippered box-type suitcase. Most importantly, with so many bags that look alike, the strap makes yours more noticeable as it pops onto the baggage carousel.

Secondly, identification tags on the outside are a given. But be sure you have a label with your name, address and phone number pasted on the inside, or use a marker and just print it somewhere inside on the bag's lining.

The ID on the inside is important because if your bag is lost or delayed, and the outside tag is torn off, the baggage clerk will ask you for items for identification on the inside. The label will be the most specific item you can give to them.

Don't forget that enlarged copy of your passport should be stored inside your bag, too.

**

Some airlines offer *Priority* baggage handling to their upper status mileage members or first class flyers. In theory this great thing to have your bags come up first.

Yes, in theory.

I find that in some airports, such as Newark and San Francisco, the tag means nothing. In fact, I have the sneaking suspicion the handlers put the 'priority' bags up last just to piss off what they think is some big-shot, snobby priority guy. Obviously, this is a routine baggage handler prank.

They don't consider that us road warriors sacrifice so much of our personal fun-time and time with our loved ones and friends and that the few perks we can cash in on are very much appreciated, especially if it helps us get home sooner.

Some years ago a priority baggage tag was issued early in the year by the airline to be used all year. I suspect that the some baggage handlers at Newark Airport would remove them. Every time I would return home, the tag would be missing.

I assumed they would steal them and then sell them to other people who did not qualify for the tag. It was not a good purchase, however, because if the passenger was to use the ill-gotten tag for a trip back to Newark, odds were it would be stolen again.

The tags would need to be replaced more than a dozen times during the year.

Currently, the priority tags are put on at bag check-in and cannot be removed unless the whole destination tag is removed. Still, they didn't come up first at Newark until recently when Continental switched to a yellow priority tag. For some reason, the yellow tags do come up a little faster.

***

As a percentage of the total, there are very few lost bags in the airline industry. Surprised? Most bags that don't show up are only delayed for a period of time. This is usually not a problem if you are on your return trip to home, unless you are scheduled for another trip in the next day or two. If that is the case, you will be like me – the proud owner of a 'backup' bag and a duplicate set of personal supplies to store in it.

I always thought that the luggage, and not the passenger, should get the frequent flyer miles. That way they would accumulate more miles a lot faster.

It is another Pepto Bismol moment when you are watching people walk away with their bags, one by one, and then you finally see the carrousel stop and your bag is still not on it.

You will then need to stand in a line of irate passengers in the same boat as you to fill out the proper forms in hopes your bag will turn up soon.

As I mentioned previously, if the bag is delayed on your trip home it's not so bad. You can easily replace some of your delayed items right out of your drawer at home and other things can usually wait the extra day or two.

When the bag doesn't arrive with you on your outbound business trip—that can be a nightmare.

It is especially bad if you are moving about after your first destination because by the time your bag arrives in that city, you may have moved on to another—then another.

Fortunately, in my experience, I have only had a delayed bag a few times and only four times on an outbound business flight. However, there was one that will stick in my mind forever.

It was a routine non-stop flight to Denver's International Airport, which left Newark in the early afternoon one fine spring day. The weather was clear as a bell and no delays were in the flight plan.

I was going to Denver to assist one of my distributors with a trade show at the convention center, which was to begin at 9:00 A.M. the following morning.

As usual I wore my jeans and a pullover golf shirt, with a decent pair of black dress shoes and a dress belt.

The plane landed on time at 5:30 P.M. but my bag apparently stopped at a bar somewhere in Newark's terminal and missed the Denver flight. So off I went to make my missing baggage report.

As I stated, bags are seldom lost but are often delayed, so I figured it would be on the next flight—and that was exactly what I was told. Supposedly, the bag would be on the next flight in from Newark that night at 11:00 P.M. and it would be delivered to my hotel. Sounded okay to me, so I wasn't very concerned.

But by 11:30 that night I was informed it apparently didn't make the flight but I was assured it was on the flight that would arrive at 1:00 A.M.

That will teach me to trust assurances from the airline.

Have you ever tried to find a store open to buy toiletries at two in the morning? Not an easy task, at least in Denver.

Just finding some local person who might even suggest something is a treasure hunt without a map. Finally, a woman pumping gas at an all night station gave me directions to a Seven-Eleven that she believed was open all night. Toothpaste, a toothbrush, deodorant, comb, hairspray and shaving supplies added up to over forty dollars, but I was set until my bag arrived the next afternoon.

Now my big problem was I didn't have a business suit for the trade show the next morning and the malls did not open until ten. I thought that if I was one of the first customers in the store, I could buy a cheap suit off the rack, a shirt and tie and be at the trade show by eleven.

I got to the mall suggested by the desk clerk at about nine-thirty and there I sat, patiently waiting for the mall to open at ten.

At ten o' clock I walked to the door but it was still locked. I peered into the building and saw an ancient security guard hobbling and slowly approaching the door to unlock it, which he finally did.

As I entered I asked him where the men's shops were and he gave me the general direction by pointing and saying, "Dat way."

There were two small men's shops and a Macy's. All of them told me the same thing; "We can have the suit ready by next week." No one seemed to understand I needed it *now*, not tomorrow and certainly not next week.

Frustrated, I left the mall planning to look stupid by going to the trade show in the same clothes I wore into town yesterday. How embarrassing, but what else could I do at that point?

Exiting out of the mall parking lot I could not make a left to go back the way I came due to a concrete center median in the road. I decided I would just go to the next traffic light and U-turn back the way I came and head to the convention center.

As I approached the traffic light I saw another group of stores on my right so I turned into the parking lot and parked in front of a Montgomery Ward store. (You non-youngsters will remember the name.)

The store was devoid of customers and I quickly found the men's department where a very helpful woman pointed me toward a rack of suites that were my size.

As I perused through the rack I noticed none of the legs were hemmed to a particular length but I finally pulled out a nice, gray pin-striped suit. It was polyester, or let's just say it was imitation wool and the price was a phenomenal seventy-five bucks.

I explained my predicament to the woman and asked if someone could just quickly hem or cuff the bottoms. She told me the tailor would not be in until tomorrow. I was about to give up again when she said, "Wait a minute. There is a Chinese dry-cleaner a few miles from here, near where I live. I heard he does excellent tailoring too. Why don't you buy the suit, if it fits, and see if he'll fix the hem? If not, you can bring it back."

"Great idea," I said to her. "And I'll need a shirt and tie."

She brought me to a table where white dress shirts were on sale for eight dollars. Amazing, and they looked okay to me. For the price, I could always use it as a rag to wash my car and it would still be a deal.

Next, I went to the rack of imitation silk ties for five bucks. That was eighty-eight dollars for my new wardrobe. No wonder they are out of business now.

With my hand written directions from the sales clerk I was off to find the Chinese tailor.

After a few turns and about five miles I saw a store with a simple sign that just said "CLEANERS," and I turned into the parking lot.

When I entered I saw a single Asian man in the work area of the shop and when he saw me he came toward the counter.

As I began to explain about the airline losing my bag and how I needed the pants fixed and perhaps the badly creased shirt pressed he began shaking his head 'no' while I was speaking. In my experience in dealing with the Asian cultures, head shaking does not necessarily mean what you may think. Many times the yes nod may only mean, "I understand you," or, "I hear you," but it may not mean, "I agree with you."

So the "no" I was seeing perhaps was only, "I have no idea what the hell are you babbling about, round eyes?"

When I was finished I said, "Please. Can you do this for me?"

"Go in room. Put on pants and jacket. I fix," he said in a not–very-friendly tone.

I went into the small rest room and put the pants on and came out.

"Put jacket on."

"No. The jacket is okay. I just need the . . ."

"Put jacket on," he demanded.

"Okay. You're the boss."

He quickly marked pant bottoms, then marked the back of the waist for adjustment and then tugged at the jacket and marked where he wanted to move the button.

I protested again and said I only wanted to fix the bottoms but he just ignored me. I surmised he was now trying to run up the tab on Yankee-Boy here who was an out-o-towner in need, and ripe to be screwed over. He continued to ignore me and said, "You give me shirt and tie. I press." Then he shooed me to the outer area to wait for the job to be done.

I asked, "How long will it take?

All he said was, "Okay. You wait."

Okay indeed. I was hooked now so I handed him the shirt and tie and went to the front of the store. I checked my wallet to be sure I had enough cash and I had a little over a hundred dollars left, so considering the deal at Wards, I resigned myself to pay the bill and accept the rip-off.

It was only about fifteen minutes before he came up to the counter with everything on hangers in plastic bags. The tie no longer had the puckered appearance and now it looked like *real* imitation silk.

"Shirt had bad seam. I fix," he told me, setting me up for the big hit on the bill.

"Great. Thanks. So how much do I owe you?" Here we go.

He looked up toward the ceiling and scratched his chin in deep calculative thought. I could see the dollar signs floating around his head.

"Tree dorrars," he said.

"What? How much?"

"Tree dorrars," he repeated in his Asian accent.

"Three dollars?" I was shocked.

"Yes. Tree dorrars."

Humph. This must be a tailor prank. I was waiting the guy to say, "No. Only screwing with you, Round Eyes. You pay hundred dorrars."

I quickly paid him and thanked him again and dashed out of the store before he changed his mind. I then headed for the hotel so I could change into my bargain suit and make it to the trade show, albeit a bit late.

At the hotel I looked in the mirror and could not believe how good the suit looked. I actually thought it looked better than the expensive suite I was waiting to arrive in my luggage. This was great and I would be less than two hours late after all the hassle.

When I got to the convention center I explained my bag still hadn't showed up and wasn't scheduled to arrive until late that afternoon. Then I told them that I just bought the suit I had on.

One of the sales guys said, "Man. I wish I could just go out and buy an Armani suit."

I laughed. "More like Armani Ward."

I then told them the whole story starting with the eighty-eight dollar bargain and concluding with the "tree dorrars" for the tailoring.

In amazement, one of the sales guys said to me, "Three bucks? Did you at least give him a ten or twenty dollar tip?"

Smiling widely, I said, "What, and spoil it for the next guy?"

***

I wore that suit a couple more times then took it to be dry-cleaned. However, when I went to pick it up the cleaners showed me how the pants fell apart. Most of the seams were glued with some sort of iron-on tape and the dry-cleaning solution dissolved the bond.

The imitation wool jacket was thread-stitched but the pressing machine melted it in several areas anyway. So my bargain Armani Ward suit was now trash. Still, it was a great deal. Besides, the airline picked up the tab for all my out of pocket costs.

***

One last thing about baggage: Train your bag to behave.

When in a crowded terminal where people are moving about in many directions, take a simple precaution to prevent someone tripping over the bag you are rolling along behind you.

Simply lift the handle a bit and hold it lower on the stem. This will pull the bag in closer behind you and you will not have someone like me falling over your bag and cursing at you.

However, when *you* fall over some inconsiderate dope's bag, try to restrain yourself from cursing and slapping the person upside the head.

Chapter 13

Trade Shows

In my career I have either attended or have exhibited at hundreds of trade shows around the U.S., Canada and in Asia. In the marketplace in which I participate the shows are all related to the electronics and high-tech industries. These include broadcast, audio and consumer electronics, along with industrial electronics and RF microwave shows. My viewpoint for trade shows is derived from experience within my particular industry, but I believe whether you are selling shoes, hardware, weapons, marbles or pet supplies, they all pretty much apply the same in principals.

These shows used to be the place where manufacturers would wait to release and show their new products to the world. Engineers or users of these products would attend to see what was new in their domains and what new "stuff" would make their lives easier or more productive. Now, with the advent of the Internet, manufacturers usually no longer wait for the annual show. They just pop the new and special product on their web site and the world can find it through search engines immediately.

Based on that, you may think then that trade shows are obsolete. Truly, in some cases they are. There has been a decline in show attendance and some shows have joined some of the airlines on the island.

The Internet is of course one reason for the decline in attendance, but another reason is 'down sizing.' If companies are short staffed and running lean, they cannot afford to send a group of people to the shows. On the positive side, if they do decide to send someone, the people that do go are usually the decision makers, the key ones you want to get into your booth.

Previously, I mentioned Comdex, which was a huge show in Las Vegas that each year drew over one hundred thousand people in attendance. The show closed its doors in 2003 and I truly think the primary reason was the Internet. It would appear that promoting all that computer technology and the associated Internet growth caused the show to not shoot itself in the foot, but in the head.

Many shows lost attendance but still have a small, but solid, draw of interested attendees. However, when exhibitors have to shell out thirty-five to fifty dollars per square foot for booth space with minimum sizes of one hundred square feet, pay hundreds, if not thousands of dollars for freight to deliver the booth materials to the convention center and back, then hundreds more to rent chairs, carpeting, tables and all other booth accessories and labor to set it up. Throw in the cost of flying personnel to the site, lodging and meals and local transportation, you need to do a hell of a lot of business to cover your costs and make a profit from the show's cost. The average show with a ten by ten foot booth costs my company around six to eight thousand with everything considered and ten grand or more if we have a larger booth.

With smaller attendance numbers many exhibitors will not renew to attend the following year. Eventually, the show declines into oblivion.

Even years ago, to make the shows fraudulently look well attended, promoters would allow students in on the last day.

Sure these young people are potential customers, but you want measurable results from the show and you cannot wait years for the branding process to get you an order such a distance down the road. Most of these students will never remember you anyway and many will never make it in their endeavored fields.

I recall one particularly lousy show in Hartford where the promoters actually went to retirement communities and rounded up busloads of seniors to walk the floors. The older folks were grabbing up any promotional items such as pens, candy or other gadgets that weren't nailed down. I had to wrestle an old woman for my display sample board of connectors that she thought would look better on her kitchen wall than in my booth. A feisty old gal she was.

A lot of trade shows now have been grouped together so attendance will be larger in total but not necessarily for the venue in which you may be participating. My company has exhibited in several shows like that. Some are worth it, if the five or six combined shows are closely related, because they will draw a percentage what I call 'crossover potentials.' But if the base of attendees that are supposed to be for your venue is very small, the additional crossovers may still not make the show worthwhile.

For example, a show in which I have exhibited in Anaheim was a West Coast technical design show related only partly to electronics and even less to my particular commodity. It has merged with a medical equipment design show, a plastics show, a show for automated contract manufacturing, a packaging machinery show and the West Coast electronics show, in which I participated in the past. Each show on its own was failing and now they appear to have a large attendance.

However, the show was marginal for my type of business so I have elected not to participate in it, at least for the next time. Sometimes it is worth trying another show in place of one or using the money to increase the size of your booth for the shows that are successful for you.

Another idea we had was to invite selected distributors to co-op a day with us. For a fee, perhaps as much as a third of just the floor space rental cost, they could send a person or two from the local region to work the booth with us. There would be no, or negligible travel expense and no lodging costs and we would usually buy them lunch or dinner. We would allow them to hand out their literature or catalogs and could sell their entire line of products except for the ones that competed with us. Then, they would get a copy of all the sales leads for that day.

We remained in control of the overall sales attempts at the booth so they wouldn't lose any potential business for us due to lack of product knowledge. It also gave our people the opportunity to teach the distributor person a little about how to sell our products.

To our advantage we can perhaps cut out one person traveling from our office and save on all of that person's expenses. Even if that is not the case, it still defrays our costs and benefits the distributor and our relationship with that distributor.

* * *

The PROPAS for trade shows differ from country to country. The U.S. has the toughest PROPAS if it is to be expected to have a successful show. PROPAS omissions can cause you to lose money and not get the number of qualified leads you expected and waste the value potential from your investment.

Oh, you're thinking, "What in Hell is he talking about? PROPAS? Never heard of it and I do shows all the time."

Yeah, well, it is my acronym for the "Proper Rules of Pain and Suffering." So read on and think about how you behave at trade shows.

Rule number one: No sitting. You are to stand for the entire time of the official show hours. If you can lean against something, good for you— it's allowed, but no sitting, and lean straight.

Rule number two: No eating or drinking in the booth. Go to the snack bar. If you are alone in the booth—suck it up and stay at the booth. This also means no restroom breaks if you are alone and no, you can't ask the person next door to you to,

"Watch my booth," or to ask for his empty coffee cup to secretly pee into. In reality, if you didn't eat or drink, as suggested, you would not need the restroom.

Rule number three: Talk to everyone who glances your way. Say "Hello," ask if they use the product you are exhibiting; get them talking to you so you can find out if they are a qualified prospect or not. If not, just tell them to piss off and don't waste your time. (Only kidding: another little prank of mine.) If you are not hoarse by the end of the day you didn't do your share of suffering or a proper job.

Rule number four: It is ten minutes before closing time on the last day of the show. Most of your neighbors are packing up because there has not been an attendee down your aisle for the last two hours and you could have set up a bowling ally in the aisle in front of your booth without fear of hitting anyone with a bowling ball. PROPAS rules insist you are required to wait until the atomic clock in Denver signals it is exactly the first second of the hour of closing time because you may have the customer that could give you a million dollar order still stop to see you.

Could happen, ya know!

I can almost hear the thoughts of you folks who have experience doing trade shows. You're thinking I am either out of my mind or playing another prank on you. Actually, both thoughts would be incorrect.

Those four PROPASs are actually true. The problem is it is almost impossible for most of us to submit ourselves to this torture in the name of business. Yes, we are a bunch of softies and it seems that all of you up and coming young people are even softer and more spoiled. So you must find a way to comply with the rules and do it by working around the pain. Here's how.

Why no sitting?

Because it appears you are not interested in the surroundings of the show or its attendees. The people walking by will glance at you, and not want to, God forbid, disturb your relaxation and disinterest in them. Even if your display attracts someone into the booth to ask you a question, and you continue to sit, it is totally disrespectful. Your body language says, "Get lost pal. I'm tired and you are nothing but a pain in the ass to me," and that is what will happen: he will get lost.

The problem with a lot of booth sales people is that the money for the show does not come out of their pockets so there is a lax attitude. What is not realized often enough is that good results afforded by correct actions could put money *into* their pockets. Let us not forget you are being paid to do your job and this is part of it. So get your ass off the chair and do it!

Here I am, a multi-decade veteran of hundreds trade shows, now with a bulging disk in my back, causing pain when I stand for a while. So what do *I* do?

High tables and stools are the answer. You can stand and lean your butt against the stool or sit while still being at eye level with the prospects. You can also turn the stool around if it has a back and put one foot on a wrung with your arms leaning over the chair-back. This will allow you to stand with some relief off of your knees and spine.

If you post yourself right up in the front of the booth, behind the high table, you can actually sit on the stool and you are ready for the eye-level contact for the 'talking part,' which I will get into in a minute.

***

The no eating rule is a must. Before you go the convention center always eat a big breakfast— it helps get you through longer. And don't drink too much coffee.

You are never to be seen chomping or chewing when a prospect may be passing by. Again, why would someone want to disturb you while you are eating just to perhaps purchase your product or service? They won't, but they will find someone who is not so busy and you will not even miss your lost target. Bad show, huh?

However, if you really need something throughout the day and have no one to relieve you from booth duty, bring a small can of nuts. Cashews are my favorite. Look up and down your aisle for a lull in attendee traffic, pop a couple of nuts, do a quick chew and swallow and your energy will rise quickly. Or, even try one of those "fun size" candy bars. This can get you through until you have an associate relieve you to go eat something at the snack bar.

Lose the gum! There is nothing more distracting to potential to see someone's wad of gum bouncing around his or her mouth

As for drinking: water is it. You can always hide a water bottle somewhere. Also, if you accidentally spill it, it will not ruin you clothes or cause stickiness or stains on any of your displays. However, if you spill it on your crotch and it looks like you wet yourself, you will find that those tall counter-tables are good crotch-covers.

***

The saying goes, "Talk is cheap," but it also can be very profitable. After all, that *is* what sales people do.

If someone looked your way there was something that caught his or her eye. Since you may not be not a Greek God or Goddess, despite what you think, it must have been something within your display. So even while they may be turning their head away, blurt out a, "Hello," or "How are you doing today?" or even something like, "How are the feet holding up?" or "Excuse me. Let me ask you what you think of this show so far." Anything will work if there is even a slight interest on their part.

If they say hello, nod and keep on going, so be it. It was just your display colors or lights hat got the glance. But if there is a product interest the "Hello" will cause them to stop and look further at what you are offering. Here is where you jump into sales mode and try to find the need and secure the lead.

Even if you discover you can't help them with their inquiry, take the lead information anyway and send literature to them. Perhaps in the future they will need your product and they will remember you.

Branding is important. They may not remember you until perhaps a rep or distributor salesperson mentions your company name and the bell clangs in the person's head: *Yeah, I heard of those people* with all positive energy behind the thought. If he sees a print advertisement or your company pops up in a Google search it will also reinforce the branding process.

"Find the need and secure the lead." Now there's a good trade show motto. That's almost as good as, "If the glove doesn't fit . . ." Never mind. I'm not going there.

***

Okay. So you are dead on your feet now on the last day and the last hour of this tortuous event and no one has been past your booth in the last two hours except for a few other exhibitor personnel on their way to the rest room.

Usually, every show's rules are you cannot begin to pack up until the show is officially closed. If you violate this rule you may not be able to attend again. If the show was horribly awful, why should you care? If you planned to scrap this show forever anyway, just get out of there as soon as you can even though you may ruin it for someone else who had a good show.

Get my drift here? Sit tight for a while. You're not the only one there and you should not ruin it for others.

Fifteen minutes before show's detonation you will see other exhibitors hurriedly putting things away as if the few extra minutes are that important. Trust me, it is not.

It is acceptable to casually put away literature except for a few copies just in case you will need them at the last minute. Additionally, you may pack away any small items such as samples or extra business cards. You also can unplug equipment that needs to cool down.

Also, you may want to return your lead retrieval machine now to beat the lines there. If someone stops at your booth after you have returned the unit, you just need to get a business card or simply write the information on the back of one of your own cards and add it to the lead download manually.

Do you think this is pie in the sky by hanging in there to the end? Most times it is. Surprisingly, I have made some great successes and money from end-of-day stoppers on their way to the exits.

Some of these can be exhibitor people. Realize that you are at this show with people who have a commonality with your marketplace, so if you are at the right show you should have some existing, as well as potential, customers exhibiting there with you. If you are any good at what you do, you will recognize this and apply your magic at the opportunity. The last day of the show is the best time to visit other booths looking for business from the exhibitors. Since it is usually a slower day, you will not be taking anyone away from trying to sell their company's products to their potential customers.

Bottom line is to follow the PROPAS as close as possible and you will pull the most value from the results of the show.

***

Trade shows can be interesting but seldom fun and seldom memorable. Oh, sure there was the time in Chicago's McCormick Place Convention Center when an attendee had a seizure in the booth next door to me and as the poor guy descended to the ground he took their pop-up type booth down with him. It left my booth neighbors in a disaster. Their graphics were creased and ruined, some of the fiberglass pieces of the pop-up booth frame were snapped in half and a piece of expensive electronic equipment on display had gotten smashed in the melee.

The man recovered quickly with only a small cut on his forehead. He got up and walked away, as if nothing happened, and without saying a word or even glancing at the mess he caused. The two people manning that booth would be in that disaster for the rest of the day, limiting their potential business results. Fortunately, that evening they would patch, repair and recover just enough to survive the rest of the show. Warriors indeed—resourceful and resilient. Pass me the duct tape, please!

There are always weird characters, wise guys, smart-asses and jerks that will turn up at your booth. It is a tiny part of the

PROPAS you must endure. There was a guy for a number of years that stopped at our booth named Nigel Earthworm. Was it his real name? I don't know but it is somewhat memorable. Does any of that make a show really memorable? Not usually.

Usually, it is something after the show closes.

Some years ago, when shows were making money, occasionally the show management would provide an evening of entertainment.

Somewhat memorable to me was the ones that were done for the Wescon Show in Anaheim, which alternated between San Francisco, then to San Jose. This was the big West Coast electronic components show and was successful for many years.

The evening of the second day of the show the show group would hire live bands, celebrity impersonators, comedians or magicians, hors d'ourves and adult beverages. It was great for a couple of hours and good for schmoozing with other exhibitors, reps and competitors.

Wescon is now extinct and many existing shows are barely squeaking by and usually can't afford this type of extra expense.

So what was really memorable for me?

That would be a show I did in San Diego at the San Diego Convention Center, of which I have no recollection of its name. How's that for memorable? I only remember it was to be a three day show and my San Diego rep firm suggested it would be good for my company to participate. They offered their assistance for booth duty and I agreed to do it. It was to be held in mid-February. That usually is a good time to leave the East Coast and head for warmer territories and San Diego is one of my favorite cities.

As typical, Monday was setup day and the show opened Tuesday.

For a first day the show was fairly busy and Gene and John from the rep firm alternated their attendance to help at the booth.

The show was to close at five o' clock that day so around four-thirty I asked the reps if they would join me for dinner that evening. I was promptly told, "Oh, no, we can't we're taking our wives out to dinner for Valentine's Day."

Oh, oh, Valentine's Day. I forgot it was February 14th and I guessed I would be in doghouse at the home front. Okay, get out of this one MacGyver!

I still had to eat dinner that night, albeit alone, so I asked where the best seafood restaurants were. Gene, my rep, gave me two recommendations but warned me that they may be busy because of all the couples out for the evening of chocolate hearts and flowers celebration.

At five o' clock I left the convention center and drove to my hotel. I quickly called Mary and apologized for forgetting V-Day. Fortunately for me she is not only very understanding but she is not very enamored with holidays created by the greeting card companies. I was off the hook for now but would make it up to her when I returned.

I was getting hungry so I headed for the first of the suggested restaurants.

It took about thirty minutes to get there due to rush hour traffic. When I arrived, I had to drive around to look for a parking space. There were none, so I created my own at the edge of a row of parked cars.

Inside was chaotic. Couples were milling about waiting for a table, the bar was packed and loudspeaker pages were being announced for various names and the host was still writing more names on the waiting list.

What the hell, I'll give it a shot. "How long is the wait?" I asked.

"Do you have a reservation, sir?"

"No. I don't."

"Oh, then it will be two or two and a half hours," was what I was told.

As I headed to the next recommended place I knew it was going to be the same situation and I was right on my premonition. The hostess just laughed at me when I told her I did not have a reservation and said, "Forget it."

I drove back to where I was staying because I remembered there was a Chili's across the street from the hotel.

The parking lot was packed there as well but I went inside anyway. There were a few teenage couples waiting for tables as I approached hostess. "Any chance for a table for one?" I asked.

This was the first time I had asked for a table for "one." The other two places probably just assumed my Valentine date was lingering somewhere in the background. Now, the truth was out. She looked at me with a strange expression and I could almost hear the loudspeakers in her brain emitting, *you loser, you. Table for one on Valentines Day? Poor bastard.* "Sure," she finally replied. "It will be about thirty minutes. What's the name? *Loser?* She was obviously thinking

"Bob," I answered, almost tempted to give an alias like, "Bond—James Bond."

After only twenty minutes the hostess' voice bellowed over the paging speakers, "Bob, party of ONE! Bob, party of ONE!"

Bob. Party of one you freaking loser!

Now, Bob, party of one, was being escorted through the restaurant with everyone, all couples, wanting to see what "Bob, party of one" looked like and why this loser had no date.

The dining area was formed in an "L" shape and as I was being lead to my table I traversed the long side of the "L." How embarrassing this was, everyone seemed to look up as I passed. Worse was when the hostess seated me at the apex of the "L" so I could look straight ahead to see everyone along area I just passed and with a slight turn of my head could see down the short portion of the "L." Unfortunately, everyone could also easily see me. Especially since the corner of the apex was raised two steps above the rest of the restaurant. I was on display.

I determined that I would never see any of these people again so I no longer cared and just shrugged it off. I was hungry and tired so screw them all. Nor was I still embarrassed.

A waiter came to the table in a minute or so and asked me what I wanted to drink, so I ordered an iced tea. Since I already looked at the menu and made a quick selection, I gave him my dinner order as well.

It had been a long day and it felt good to sit and relax a bit. Since I cannot see well either close-up or distance without glasses, I took them off for the first time that day and began rubbing my eyes with the heels of my hands. It felt good to massage my tired eyelids and my slight headache.

I heard, "Here you go, sir," and a "thunk" as the waiter placed a large glass of iced tea in front of me. I stopped rubbing my eyes, blinked a few time trying to clear the haziness of my vision and looked at the tall blurry glass of dark amber liquid. I had become very thirsty.

I reached for the glass and as I brought it up to my mouth for a thirsty gulp I felt a terrible pain somewhere in back of one eye. My head involuntarily whip-lashed backward but the pain still pursued. Slamming the glass roughly on the table I suddenly I realized something was in my nose.

I grabbed fiercely at my face and felt a plastic shaft—a large straw— and pulled it out of my nostril. Since the end was pinched somewhere between the back of my eyeball and my now bewildered and perhaps partially damaged brain, it had held and air-locked a quantity of the iced tea inside the oversized diameter straw. As I pulled it out of my nose, ice tea flowed all over my crotch and it appeared that I had wet myself.

Cursing, tossing the now booger-ized straw on the table, then reaching for a napkin and my glasses, I struck the tea glass and almost spilled it but I caught it clumsily and only spilled about a third of its contents.

With my glasses back on and napkin in hand drying my crotch I noticed that there were a great deal of people watching my antics. Some were chuckling; others appeared to be dumbstruck by Loser Bob's performance and others were shaking their heads in disgust thinking, what an asshole! Then everyone knew, or at least thought they knew, the reason why I was alone that evening.

Embarrassing? Sure. I couldn't help starting to laugh at myself; I must have looked so absurd. I guess that when the people saw me laughing all by myself, and not understanding I was actually laughing at myself, they surely thought I was a nut case.

The damned straw was on the table and now that my glasses were on, I saw it was totally clear. I don't mean translucent, or a bit cloudy; this straw was crystal clear.

So it was the old *Invisible Straw* prank that SOB waiter pulled on me. Oh well, it goes into my history as a classic and will always be memorable.

When I was ready to leave I paid in cash so no one would know my real name: Bond—James Bond.

***

Foreign trade shows disobey most all the PROPAS concepts, especially the Asian ones.

Taiwan trade shows are a scream. The exhibitors appear to be there on some type of punishment detail their company has served upon them. No one looks happy, no one smiles and few will pay attention to you.

As you walk the aisles you will often see five or six people crammed into a ten foot wide booth not only eating, but cooking some nasty smelling, non-descript, mystery things on an electric burner. They will shove wads of the unrecognizable slop into their mouth with chopsticks while samples of their meal are displayed proudly on their chin and clothing. Belching and spitting out shells, bones and other food debris is normal during mealtime in Asia. Farting is acceptable as well while eating. Pretty disgusting.

Needless to say, you don't want to disturb these people while engaged in their feeding frenzy, but if you do stop in an attempt to get information, you will be ignored. Great for business, huh?

Sitting is more common than standing in Taiwan and other Asian shows. Usually, there will be a little round table in the booth and if they are not eating, you may be invited into the booth to sit at the table and discuss your interests. But if it is anywhere near feeding time, forget about it.

There is one PROPAS that I didn't find the need to mention for U.S. shows and that is "No Sleeping." Yeah, some ambitious booth personnel will sleep at the booth during the show.

The funniest thing I saw was a Taiwanese man sleeping in a chair in his booth. The chair was turned so his back was aligned with the aisle. His head had tipped backward and was all the way back with his face to the ceiling, and was sticking out into the aisle. Eyes closed, his mouth was wide open, and he was snoring.

As one Taiwanese attendee was passing by he smiled at the sleeper, looked at his companion with a devilish expression and flicked his cigarette ash into the guys gaping mouth. There was a slight hiss as the ash hit the tongue but the sleeper never missed a snore. He did however, click his tongue and swallow a couple of times to dilute the ash with a little saliva. Now his mouth was black and looked like an ashtray but, undisturbed, he continued his nap.

Some European shows have exhibitors that will sometimes have elaborate events of serving food and champagne. This reminds me of the old days when the company I worked for at the time, participated in shows which electrical contractors attended. The show management would advertise that "Free Hot Dogs and Beer" would be served at the show. When the beer and dogs were announced, there would be no one looking at the displays. Everyone, including a lot of exhibitors, flocked to the chaotic beer fest. Then, after kegs of beer were drained and enough hot dogs to supply a baseball stadium were consumed, the aisles were full of glassy-eyed drunks belching and leaving the show.

Some exhibitors of U.S. shows still may do the party thing, but usually for an hour after the show closes—much better that way.

***

One last suggestion to consider: since most shows are in major cities, nightlife can be very tempting to partake in. This is okay for the last day of the show, that is drinking and keeping late hours, but you need to be fresh and clear-headed if you are booth duty the next morning.

I know it is a sacrifice for some of you, especially if the trade show is in Las Vegas, but don't do it. Have dinner, a drink and make it back to your room by eleven and I can assure you will never get cigarette ashes flicked into your mouth.

Chapter 14

Humor

A good sense of humor, as noted earlier, is a necessity. If you can make light of some stressful situations if makes them less stressful and if you can laugh at some silly things that happen, like a straw up your nose, it just makes the day go by easier and smoother.

Please don't confuse *jokes* with *humor*. Sure they are intertwined but not the same. What may be a funny joke to your sense of humor may be an insult to the person you tell it to. And if you choose to tell it to your customer or client, you better be prepared for an unexpected reaction. Unless you know the person very well, I suggest you limit your joke telling.

For example: tell a joke about a drunk and you may not know that the listener may be an alcoholic, or, perhaps his brother, the drunk, just died from liver disease caused by alcohol. Blond jokes are all the rage, but maybe the person's blond daughter just washed out of college because she was not too bright, or just backed out of the garage without opening the door. Worse yet, is starting a joke with the phrase, "Did you hear the one about the [Christian], [Jew], [Asian], [Black], [Mexican], [Polack], [Irishman] Etc.," can be a kiss of death to you in a customer relationship if the joke insults the person.

I learned this lesson when I was a young rookie salesman in the 1960s. I had a great phone rapport with a buyer for a large company and I did a lot of business with him. I spoke to him almost every day for close to a year and felt I knew him very well. His last name had a lot of C's, Z's and Y's in it and it was of a Slavic or Eastern European origin.

One day I started with the, "Did you hear the one about the black guy who . . ." I can't remember the joke and it wasn't really bad, but yes it would be considered racist today.

I closed the punch line and laughed myself but didn't hear a sound from the other end of the line. "Carl? You there?" I asked.

Carl spoke softly and said, "You never met me did you?" My stomach sank. *Oh shit. Now I did it.*

I began babbling and apologizing and didn't know where this was going. Suddenly, Carl broke out in hysterical laughter. He laughed so hard it sounded like he couldn't breathe, until finally he gained control of himself and told me, "I got you good!" He told me he was an Eastern European white guy but decided to play that trick on me. Not to teach me a lesson, no, that was not in his thoughts al all. It was *his* sense of humor poking this prank at me.

That sent a serious message to me, which shaped the style of any joke telling I did from that point on. Actually, I try to not tell 'jokes' at all, unless they are clean, and could not offend anyone, anyplace or anything. Although there are a few open targets that most people will feel is okay, they could still come around and bite you in the backside. Self-deprecating jokes are okay, but then you may reduce the respect your customer may have for you. Politicians deserve a joke or two, but if you tell it to some one who happens to be on the political side of the one you are poking fun at, it could be disastrous.

When I presented a whole day seminar, I knew I had to keep people from falling asleep. Keeping people involved with a lot of eye contact and questions, doing some hands-on things, and carrying a water pistol that was used to threaten to squirt anyone caught with their eyes closed forced attentiveness in the audience. I would interject some wit and humor to keep 'em laughing, and if it worked, I would use it again another time in another meeting.

By the end of the day I would tell a story that I developed from an old joke I had heard. It fit the scenario and would not insult anyone, or so I thought. It went like this: "I have to thank you all for attending today and I want to leave you with a story about my grandmother. Grandma was a great woman. She was smart, tenacious and taught me most of what I know to survive the riggers of daily life, especially in the business world. She was a tiny, frail, but no-nonsense woman and was not to be discounted—ever.

One day Grandma walked into the bank with a large paper bag full of twenties, fifties and hundreds. She plopped the bag of cash down at the teller's window and said, 'I want to make a deposit, young man.'

The teller looked at the bag, noted a lot of the bills were crumpled and jammed into the bag. He asked, 'Where did you get all this cash?'

'That's not your business young man,' she said.

Already intimidated by this five-foot-one, feisty old woman, he stammered, 'Well, uh, we need to know.'

'No you don't. Get your boss here,' grandma snapped back.

After the same conversation with the teller's supervisor, the floor manager and the branch manager, and a few others, Grandma would still not say how she obtained the cash. She was finally escorted into the office of the bank president. The bag of cash was placed on his desk and as he glanced at the bag, said, 'Mrs. B., we really know where you got all this money.'

Realizing she was at the end of the challenge, and was not any further along, Grandma relented, 'If you must know, I bet a little bit.'

The stuffy banker smiled and said, 'Oh, I see. You won it gambling.'

'I don't gamble,' she replied. 'I said, I bet a little.'

The look on the banker's face expressed he did not understand, so Grandma proceeded to give him an example. 'How about this? I'll bet you ten thousand dollars that by noon tomorrow your testicles will be perfectly square.'

The banker laughed. 'That's ridiculous, Mrs. B.'

'Then take the bet,' Grandma replied.

Thinking that the bet *was* ridiculous, but perhaps this just might be a quick ten grand he could take from this obviously crazy old woman, he stood, extending his hand to shake on the deal, saying, 'You're on.'

Grandma left and the banker ordered two of his security guards to sentinel his office door. Then, at closing, he had an armored car take him home and again, and two armed security men guarded him the entire night. The next morning he was driven to the bank in the armored car and had more guards posted at his office door waiting for noon.

At three minutes before noon, Grandma entered the banker's office with another well-dressed gentleman carrying a briefcase. The banker hoped his ten thousand was in the briefcase. 'Sorry to say, Mrs. B., you've lost the bet.'

'If you think I would take your word for it sir, you're mistaken. I need to inspect the merchandise,' Grandma said, as the man she came in with had a confused look on his face as if he knew not what was going on.

The banker protested. 'Mrs. B., I'm the bank president. I just can't . . .'

"We're talking about a lot of money here. I need to inspect," Grandma interrupted.

The banker thought a moment and realized she was right and certainly wanted the ten thousand dollars. He stood, dropped his trousers, then his boxers. Grandma approached for a closer look, then reached over and scooped hold of the man's testicles for inspection. With that, the man she brought with her dropped to his knees with his hands to his face and began yelling, 'No! No! No!' in a panicky voice.

The banker, now a bit frightened, asked, 'What's wrong with him?'

'Oh, nothing,' Grandma replied casually. 'It's just that I bet you ten thousand yesterday that your testicles would be square and I lost that bet. But I bet him one hundred thousand dollars, that by noon today, I would have the president of Bank of America, right by the balls.'"

This story always evoked raucous laughter. Once it subsided I concluded with, "And the moral of the story is: You sometimes have to give up a little to gain a lot. Grandma gave up ten thousand to gain ninety. Today you gave up a little of your time and I am sure you have gained knowledge today, and will gain a lot in sales commissions as you use that knowledge."

Pretty neutral, huh? Maybe so, but when I was invited to do an hour and a half training session at a annual meeting for a new distributor in Massachusetts it didn't go very well.

I should have known the karma was bad when I checked into the hotel in Springfield the night before and the clerk looked at me and said, "Cootie?"

"What?"

"Are you a Cootie?" he asked.

"No," I said. "Are you a cockroach?"

He explained to me the hotel was hosting the National Cootie Convention, which is some organization within the VFW. The attendees for that convention were wearing red shirts with logos of the old Cootie game on it. This was a kids game from years ago that would allow you to build a big plastic bug, a piece at a time, in order to win. Strange logo for a VFG group, I thought.

The next morning, I was wrapping up the short session to about fifty people and I decided to throw in the *Grandma* story. The delivery was smooth and well practiced. When I finished the punch line, no one laughed. No one! I did see a couple of guys that were suppliers like me with their hand covering their mouths, but not a chuckle could be heard. I was stumped. Was this a planned prank?

I had finished just before the lunch break and decided to take my presentation materials out to my car. While loading my trunk, one of the other suppliers, doing the same, smiled at me and said, "Tough crowd, huh?"

I asked him what the deal was with these people and was told, "You'll see."

Returning to the hotel's banquet room for the luncheon I was to be seated at one of the tables for six people, about room center, in front of the long Head Table.

The company's president called the luncheon to order and thanked everyone for attending and noticeably tossed me a nasty look. He then proceeded to present a few sales awards to some employees. I began to wonder if we were ever going to eat lunch. I was starving and I wanted to head back to New Jersey right after lunch—about a five hour drive. Oddly, each presentation was ended with a, "and may God bless you," statement to the recipient.

Finally the presentations were finished and I figured we now would eat.

Not yet.

First, the Right Reverend Willy Bob Brimstone was to give the invocation, then say grace. He did this for another thirty minutes by spewing Hell-fire and brimstone quotes and how the evil people (like me, I guess) will be damned to an eternity in Hell. He stared at me when he said this. I figured at this point I was doomed at this company so I would let them pay for my lunch and I'd get out of Dodge.

The entire company was made up of religious extremists. Who knew? It was a job requirement to work there. That's okay by me, but there are two things that should not be mixed with business: religion or politics. These can both be volatile subjects and can destroy any seller/buyer relationship—like I just had done.

Since I was ignored while eating, when finished I just left.

A week later I received a scathing letter about how vulgar and disrespectful I was and was told they would never buy my product again. I was not going to cry about this one. Since I was offended too by the way they treated me after the meeting I figured it wasn't worth any effort to kiss butt. I would probably say "shit" or "damn" one day and get banished anyway. I felt that if they didn't like my grandma, to hell with them too.

They are gone today. Why? I wonder. They had gone out of business only a couple of years later.

As you can see, no matter what you intend to joke about, you need to know your audience and that is not always possible. I bet I have pissed off a few people with some of my comments in this book. But the time has come in my life where I do not need to worry if someone is too sensitive to carry on with his or her life because of something I have said. Get over it and move on! Throw out the book if you choose.

So, did you hear the one about handicapped, Polish, Jewish sailor trying to get into the Pearly Gates and Saint Peter asked—?

Forget about it. I haven't been there since the '60s.

Chapter 15

The Asian Experience

Eastern Culture is something most of us in the West do not fully understand. Here in the United States we are so diversified that we have lost most of the culture and history of our original heritage. Oh, sure, we say things like we are German-American or Irish-American or African-American, and the like, but the thing is—we are all still Americans.

Most of us are not *all* German or *all* Irish or other. Most of us are mixed with many other nationalities and even other races. Very few of us are pure to our heritage unless we have just crept across the border last week illegally.

So what is the problem with this? Not a damned thing!

We are Americans and that means a mix of many nations' people—or perhaps not a mix, but it doesn't matter either way.

We keep some of our ancestor's customs and culture and many times religious beliefs and apply them to family life.

However, outside the family we are pretty much just plain old Americans.

That is why I am not an advocate of the latest politically correct "multiculturalism" as it is referred to in the context of encouraging new immigrants not to blend into the majority-population's traditions that have been upheld since this country's inception. I believe multiculturalism, as it is now defined, separates us as Americans and forces us into groups that can be at odds with, or even fear or hate each other.

Same for language. This country was founded on English and as people came here they learned the language to assimilate into their new American culture. I would think a majority of Americans might feel the same as me. If you don't, I'm not offended. If *you* are, for some unfounded reason, so be it. I can't help that.

English is still the international business language, as well as the global language for airline pilots. If a Chinese speaking person needs to do business in France or Germany, they will use English as a common ground and pilots flying internationally do the same.

As you might have deduced, I am not one of the politically correct thinkers nor am I afraid to say what I believe. As Rodney King said, "Why can't we just all get along?" The answer to that is because too many people are trying to tell others how to think and what to think. I believe this impedes our personal freedoms and beliefs. You think what you want and I'll do the same. I won't try to force my beliefs upon you and you do the same with me. Only then, Rodney, can we all get along.

I am sure, that there are those who will read this and call me racist or bigot or some other insult. This is only because I may not agree with them, or they with me. Since that is not true, I say, as Rhett Butler in *Gone With The Wind* said, "Frankly Charlotte, I don't give a damned." Think what you like. You want to call me names . . . well, the old sticks and stones thing applies. I'm not bothered.

Now that that's off my chest and sets up the next statements, I will tell you that most Asian cultures and family names go back for thousands of years without change. And it appears many Asians do not often mix cultures as we do in the West. Koreans don't usually immigrate to Japan and Japanese usually don't marry Chinese—at least in their native countries.

The "Original" people of Taiwan are believed to have migrated from Southeast Asian countries, even the Philippines. So the "Originals" were a mixture then blending with Chinese. Thereafter, people from Mainland China arrived but didn't often merge with the original people. The Originals can be compared with our Native American people and were displaced by the new Chinese immigrants. The Originals, like the American Indian, have settled in various enclaves about the island.

I have noticed that Taiwanese people usually don't have a lot of Vietnamese or Indonesian buddies but they do have Filipino maids and handymen. In fact, Taiwanese people believe that even Mainland Chinese people are of different a culture and many frown upon mixed marriages of the two.

So are they racist or bigoted? I don't know, because they don't care what others think and if they discriminate without forethought it's usually because their forefathers from the beginning of history did and I guess that is a freedom of preference that they have. It becomes *their* culture. To them, there is nothing wrong with it. I cannot find one Asian that is 'sensitive,' as we call it, about another Asian country's lack of love for them unless it becomes a fear of invasion.

In my questioning about this I was told their traditions are to be keep within their own culture so not to dilute the traditional thinking and customs that has been handed down through the centuries. There were a few who told me that there is no problem with the mixing of different cultures from other nations. However, when I asked if their family has married into other cultures I was told no. Either way, this works for them. Agree or not, that is the way it is.

Sure, there are some that do marry and mix, but usually they are the ones who moved to the U.S. and settle where no one notices or cares.

Fortunately, or consequently, however you view it, their culture is strong and very traditional. Asians in general have strong family ties, respect for the old, strong work ethics and demand a lot from their children regarding education and respect for their elders. I see nothing wrong with that. In fact, I applaud it.

***

So what is so different about Asia?

Taiwan is the country I most often visit so I'll start there.

I have accumulated a list of Taiwan tips but they also apply to China as well and perhaps even more so.

Two Basic rules will get you through everything:

1. Always watch your step. Literally.
2. When eating, NEVER ask, "What is this?"

Miscellaneous Things to Remember

1. There is no tough enforcement of public safety standards.
    a. UL, CSA, ASA, ANSI, OSHA, and DIN are modern names for some Chinese children, not standards.
2. The words, "Drive Safely" do not translate into Chinese.
3. First rule of driving: "There are no rules of driving."
4. Motor bikes use sidewalks (see 6)
5. Automobiles use sidewalks (see 6)
6. Pedestrians do not have the right of way. (Or any other rights. See 4 & 5)
7. Never assume public rest rooms have toilets or towels.
8. Table manners are an American thing.
9. In Taiwan, the phrase, "Here's looking at you," comes from your dinner plate.
10. KTV is not a TV station.
11. Pin-do-nuts are not donuts.
12. Sea Cucumbers are not cucumbers.
13. "American" sandwiches, coffee, breakfast or any American-style-stuff isn't even close.

14. Interesting menu items: Shlimp, Robster, Beam Curb, krad, (crab)Tenpura, Bacoon, Chocolate Dirt. Spelling on menus sometimes mix up lower case 'b's' and 'd's'. Adalone, adbuctor, (a type of clam) enchilaba or string deans are common on menus.
15. Beds are made from butcher-block wood.
16. Current hit songs in nightclubs: How Much is that Doggie in the Window, (about supermarket shopping, no doubt) Ol' Cotton Fields Back Home (ridder biddy baby in Rooweezeeana) and Moon Liver. Not kidding here at all.
17. "Good Morning!" means "hello" any time of day or night.
18. In food items, "fish" means *anything* or parts of *anything* that was once in the sea.
19. Swastikas are religious symbols and "nigga" is a Chinese slang word, not a racial slur.
20. Important: 7-11s (and there are plenty of them) carry Dove Bars or Häagen Dazs. But still, always bring beef jerky.
21. Most importantly, don't forget to bring your Pepto Bismol! You can't buy it there.

More Observations

22. There are a lot of three legged dogs. (See 3)
23. Handicapped access does not exist. If you didn't pay note to 3, 4, 5, & 6, they believe you deserve what you get.
24. That sewage smell in basement parking garages is sulphur due to geothermal activity. If on the street, it *is* sewage.
25. Night markets are an experience.
26. McDonald's, Burger King, TGI Friday's, Hooters, are some of the American chains. Don't expect the same as USA.
27. However, Ruth's Chris in Taipei is as good as USA.
28. Garbage trucks play music-box style Brahms, Beethoven or Bach when stopped to pick up trash.

***

The very first time I got off the plane at Taipei's Chiang Kai-Sheck Airport, (CKS) the first sign I saw was not "Welcome to Taiwan, ROC."

What I saw was a very large sign in bold red letters warning: "The smuggling of illegal drugs, narcotics or guns into Taiwan, Republic of China, is an offence punishable by death." Yeah, Dorothy, you're not in Kansas anymore.

You will then clear immigration and customs and your associate will meet you at the main terminal and you will then begin your drive into the city itself. As you enter the two-lane speedway that will eventually connect with the east – west freeway toward Taipei City, there may be a driver behind you that feels your driver is driving too slowly.

Now, since your driver is doing nearly seventy miles per hour and will not move over for the Mercedes which is right on his bumper, you may think Mister Mercedes will honk his horn, flash his high-beams and flip your associate the Chinese Tweedy Bird. But no—that's not the way it's done.

Exceeding seventy miles per hour, the Mercedes will pull up and bump the back of the car you are in. Not to be upset, your driver will utter a few grumbles in Mandarin dialect and either speed up or slow down. Either way, he will get bumped again until he moves over into the other lane.

When he does, the Mercedes will cruise past, not even glancing over, as if nothing happened and your driver will do the same.

So, you ask, what about the police?

Once while riding on the freeway, sitting in the passenger seat, the car in front of us suddenly stopped short. Lee, my Taiwanese associate, who was driving, crashed into the back of that car.

As this happened, my left hand was thrust forward and a few of my finger nails were lifted up when hitting the cell phone holder on the center console. I assumed it was a new form of Chinese torture, and it would have surely worked if I had some secret to tell. I wrapped my bloodied fingers in a handkerchief and got out of the car.

The problem was caused by a driver of a white Porsche who saw three young girls whose car was stopped off to the side of the road. He didn't bother to pull off to the side as well; he just slammed on the brakes and stopped in the first lane.

The vehicle behind him was able to stop before hitting him but Lee was following too close and wasn't as lucky; he crashed into the second car.

Everyone was out of his or her cars yelling and jabbering and pointing at my now red handkerchief when a police officer pulled up and got out of his patrol car.

More staccato jabbering, yelling, pointing to my hand and other animated gestures ensued with the police officer listening and just nodding his head to the affirmative. Then suddenly everyone, including the cop, got back into their vehicles and drove off.

I was amazed. The officer never asked to see a driver's license or insurance card, never issued a summons or warning to the genius that caused the accident. He just listened to all the shouting, nodding his head. Then got back into his car at the same time as everyone else and disappeared.

Another time, again as a passenger, we were the first car stopped at a traffic light in the far right lane of a "Y" intersection. The two right lanes were to use the right fork and of course the left two lanes were for the left side.

A motorbike pulled up to the right front fender of my associate Wu's car and held onto it so he wouldn't have to put his feet on the street. Now, if that was my car and some clown decided to lean on it, the Jersey guy in me would have had me yelling at him to get his greasy paws off my car. Wu didn't seem to even notice.

When the light turned green, the genius on the bike intended to spring ahead and cross the two right lanes so he could jet his way up the road to the two left lanes. Needless to say, he didn't make it.

As Wu also darted forward he hit the bike with his left front bumper and headlight and the bike and its driver hit the pavement.

Wu got out of the car and again, the two drivers yelled at each other, Wu pointing to his broken headlamp and the biker pointing to his dented and road-scraped motorbike. Then Wu got back in the car and the biker got on his bike and proceeded to almost get hit again by another car. We then were on our way as if nothing happened.

Insurance? Sure they have it. But I was told it is cheaper to repair the car yourself then to make a claim, then pay the higher insurance rates. Why even get it?

I also assume that lawyers don't do very well in Taiwan. Wow, what a treat that is.

***

In most Asian countries traffic is a major experience. No matter if you are the driver, the passenger, or worse, the poor pedestrian trying to cross the street, you risk your life at all times.

Rules of the road may exist somewhere but it seems no one knows what they are. And if they do exist, no one follows or enforces them. There is no cause for concern to drive on the wrong side of the road if you are in a hurry and can get around traffic that way. Or, maybe go up the OFF ramp of the freeway because you happen to be on the wrong side of the road to go up the ON ramp. And how about the old drive-on-the-sidewalk trick? That's a very common one.

The cities are choked with this lunatic traffic—most of it is motorbikes; literally millions of motorbikes whiz around the cities because they are cheap, don't use much gas and can be parked in rows of hundreds on sidewalks.

It is quite a sight to watch as motorbike after motorbike collects into a mob-scene at a red traffic light. Most of the bikers, or maybe they are bandits, wear surgical masks of varying designs and colors. They have either just held up a bank, or this is to keep dirt, fumes and city-soot out of their lungs while driving. Also, when they run your ass over in an intersection you cannot identify them.

Because many major city intersections do not allow left turns, dozens of motorbikes will swoop a right-hand turn into the crosswalk, then an immediate half U-turn and stop at that traffic light. Here is where pedestrians are in mortal danger. As you may be trying to legally cross the street, perhaps as many as forty to fifty motorbikes are whizzing around you to line up for that now straight run as a replacement for the not-allowed left turn.

As I said, pedestrians have no right of way.

When I refer to 'motorbikes' I am implying more like motor scooters or mini-bikes. There are very few Harley hog's or Suzuki crotch rockets here. These are vehicles strictly for practical, economical transportation.

You will sometimes see entire families on one of those little bikes. Once I saw a woman driving a scooter type bike with a flat platform floor at her feet. She had a kid, perhaps about five, standing in front of her between the handlebars. There was a two-year-old on her lap and a baby in her backpack carrier. Her husband was riding sidesaddle on the rear fender package carrier and their three legged dog tri-plodded alongside trying to keep up. Of course, no one wore a helmet. I wonder how you say, "We don't need no stinkin' helmet!" in Chinese.

Three-legged dogs are common in Taiwan and China. I believe it is traffic related but I've often wondered if sometimes the dog was the victim of someone who needed a quick snack. And yes, they still do eat dog meat in Taiwan and China but supposedly only in the more remote backcountry regions.

And no, I have never tried it.

But other strange foods abound. As you traverse about the area you may see a MacDonald's, a Burger King, Hooters or some other American chain restaurant. Don't think it is going to be the same as you may be used to. Oh, sure, it's close but not the same.

Bring a person from Taiwan or China to a Chinese restaurant in the U.S. and ask them what they think about Americanized Chinese food and they will tell you, with an expression of disgust, "It not same." I don't think the word "sucks" translates to Chinese, otherwise they would use it.

Burgers don't taste like beef . . . hmmm, maybe I have eaten doggie.

Hooters should be called Mini Hoots, if you get my drift. And the Buffalo wings are really bad.

There seems to be a Seven Eleven on every block and they do sell Dove Bars and Häagen Dazs, which are as good as anywhere else and a lifesaver if you're desperate for something good and forgot to pack your U.S.-made beef jerky.

One place that is equal to the U.S. grade of preparation and flavor was the Ruth's Chris Steakhouse in Taipei. The steak was certified U.S. beef and it was prepared in the same manner as in the U.S. It was great, but very expensive.

However, if you have someone local taking you to dinner, allow them to take you to where *they* would go. You will experience the true local culture of the foods. The primary foods are vegetables, fish and chicken. Then, duck, pork and some things that may or may not be from the either the animal or vegetable worlds.

When I first started visiting Taiwan I usually stayed at a traditional Chinese style hotel. That is, a Spartan room with a bed as hard as the earlier mentioned Connecticut bed-board incidents. My first experience caused me so much back pain I had housekeeping underlay the bottom sheet with ten folded blankets to add some softness. It didn't work and they though I was nuts.

When I went to the breakfast buffet the first delight I saw was what I call 'guppies and beans.' A guppy, as you may know, is a tiny fish and the beans were a string bean-like veggie. The fish are whole: head, eyes, innards and fins and they are simply dried and tossed into the beans. Actually, they are not bad, but for breakfast—not my type of Cheerios.

Then there is congie, a gruel from rice water, tofu, some tiny boiled egg not from a chicken, some very pale-yoke fried eggs from what appears to be a sick chicken and many mystery foods that do nothing for my pallet nor fill my stomach.

Traditional Chinese dining is okay but must be done with an open mind and a willingness to experience new things . . . along with a strong stomach.

Even the best of restaurants will have something to gross you out. For example, at a high-end buffet there was a huge variety of foods, many of which were what you would see in U.S. buffets. There were delightful trays of whole steamed fish, which is 'whole' like the guppies, only larger, and are intact as when they came out of the sea, missing only the hook or net.

If you are one of the early ones to attack the fish and pull off the treasured 'cheek,' which is behind the gill, or a nice piece from the back, you will enjoy it immensely. If you arrive to the steam tray after someone has torn off the head, which is a delicacy, or someone has broken open the stomach cavity, then the remainder of that fish's byproducts is not going on my plate.

Some other items in that buffet were a little unusual. Chicken kidney and sheep parts did nothing to whet my appetite. I didn't have the interest to ask what "parts" they were. I can bet they weren't lamb chops.

Desserts are usually labeled in English and my favorite is 'Chocolate Dirt.' They are chocolate sprinkles for your ice cream.

Lunch at a seafood restaurant is fun. You get to see all the menu items alive in tanks. You will select your fare, it will be captured and it will be prepared for you however you request it.

Once I ordered a fish to be prepared sashimi style. The fish came out on a bed of crushed ice, gutted with head and tail removed. Then it was sliced into sections of sashimi and was replaced back into a body-form, where the skin was underneath in one strip on the ice. That's okay too. However, the ol' chef's prank was to stick the head and tail vertically into the crushed ice at the appropriate ends of the body. Interestingly, the eyes and mouth of the fish were still moving and the tail was twitching pretty rapidly. Now that's fresh! But even my female Taiwanese associate couldn't handle it and asked to have the head and tail taken away.

Would you like a doggie bag for that, lady?

Sorry, I mean fishy bag, Doggie is not on the menu today.

***

One fine evening my Taiwanese associates took me to dinner to one of the best restaurants in Taipei. It was atop a fifty-floor skyscraper office building and had a beautiful view. The fare was to be a ten-course ultra gourmet dinner and the place was very upscale. Ivory chopsticks with silver tips were prominently placed at every seat along with a crystal glass and some fine bone-china dishware. The linen and lace that adorned each table seemed a bit of over-kill in my opinion and looked out of place despite the ivory chopsticks.

The menu was printed in both Chinese and in English. There were words like robster and schlimp, sea cucumber, seaweed, dachshund and so on. They seem not to have an English proof reading service available, which is not uncommon in most restaurants and other public places catering to international guests.

The salad course was interesting. Some shredded greens, not like any lettuce I ever had, was topped with a crispy crouton made from the deep-fried gnarly skin of a chicken's foot. Tiny unnerving scales were visible but fortunately no talon-nails were included in this dish. Whole feet are reserved for other dishes that include the little toe knuckles and the dirty toenails— I mean talons.

The subsequent courses were also interesting but not very flavorful.

Around course seven a fancy stemmed glass and stainless steel cup, in which an ice cream sundae may be served, was placed in front of me. It was filled with a white sauce and some pink things were submerged in it. They looked and tasted like rubber bands. I then made the stupid mistake of asking, "What is this?"

"We tell you later," one said with a grin on his face.

"No. Tell me now," I insisted.

"No. We tell you later."

"Look. I don't care if it's monkey brains or worse, I just want to know what it is."

"Fish. It's fish," he said, smiling.

Knowing that Taiwanese and Chinese people will call a snail, a snake, a clam or a walrus turd a 'fish' as long as it came out of the ocean, I said, "That's not fish. What kind of fish?"

"Okay. That's sea cumber"

Cucumber? Doesn't look like a vegetable and it's not green. I don't get it, I thought.

I then was told that a sea cumber is a large sea slug; a giant living greenish slimy creature with wart-like bumps on it like a cucumber. But I still didn't see the resemblance of the description to what I was eating.

I shrugged and said, "Well it doesn't look like a slug *or* a cucumber."

They laughed again.

"What?" I said suspiciously.

"We tell you later."

"Dammit, stop it. Tell me now," I demanded.

"Okay. That's part where waste passes through," I was informed.

Nice. Why didn't the menu just say, *Course seven: Assholes of Sea Cucumber?* I could have ordered a double.

The last course was the best. "Here's looking at you!" was the motto. A small bowl of fish eyeballs in a slippery sauce was the final fare. Mmmm, good.

The only problem was those confounded silver-tipped, non-grip chopsticks were almost impossible to grab and hold onto the little orbs. Every time I thought I had one in the grip of my sticks the thing would fire out like a watermelon seed squeezed between your fingers. One rocketed over the top of the bowl, just missed the waiter's pant leg and rolled under an adjacent table to perhaps to look up the woman's dress that was seated there.

Finally mastering the trick to grasp one, I discovered the gelatinous, fishy-salty flavor was not too unpleasant after you got over the disgusting pop it made in your mouth when you bit into it.

After a few trips to Taiwan you get used to things with heads and innards in tact, the chicken feet, either fried skins or toes-and-all-whole feet. And sautéed, black chicken (and I mean the meat is black) served in its entirety with head, neck and feet, but no feathers or innards.

Another time a regular chicken was delivered to the table on a rack, standing there in its entirety, looking like it was ready to do a tap dance. The head was in tact although the eyes were popped and dried out during cooking. I asked Joseph, my host, who would eat the head—joking, of course. He said his wife likes the neck and she proceeded to separate it from the body and the head. My fourteen-year-old mentality seized my brain and I lost my adult control. I picked up the head and poked my index finger into the remaining neck and began to use it as a finger puppet saying "hello" in a high voice as I had it looking at the people at the table.

Yes, they laughed. Fortunately, they know and understand my sense of humor. *(Crazy American.)*

Whole fish, eyes and many other unusual food items complement the standard vegetables, rice or noodles (or the singular 'Noodle' as it is called) served with these main dishes. Still, bring along beef jerky so you can substitute for the things you just will not eat.

The one thing that does bother me is restaurants in some areas will practice some unsanitary and rather disgusting things. For example they may hang plucked ducks by the neck at various spots around their parking lot. Ducks hanging on street signs, poles, building awnings and even on the side mirrors of a truck, are not unusual. Oddly, flies and birds don't seem to bother the hanging carcasses too much. I don't know if this is a drying process, aging process or simply for attempting to collect fly larva but I was sure not to order duck that day.

The one thing that I was amazed at was when I saw several of those blue painter's tarps spread out next to a driveway of an unpaved parking lot in an industrial area; they were covered with strips of drying fish.

The strips were being dusted with the dry, black, previously oil-soaked driveway-dirt as our vehicle drove past. The good news was by driving past so closely, it did frighten away the birds and two cats that were feasting on the fish.

Board of Health? Not here, my friend. And I would bet the finished dish tasted great and no local would ever get sick.

There are some restaurants that serve small sea cucumbers along with the antipasti type appetizers. They do look like cucumbers when they are whole, but because of the tiny size they looked like little gherkins. I refuse to eat these mainly because I cannot pick them up with chopsticks. It is like trying to pick up a glob of phlegm; it just oozes away and you will lose your appetite quickly anyway. Lugies are not in my list of favorite snacks.

You may even discover a place that serves rough-cut French fries. Oh, but then you notice a small black dot on both sides at one end. Fries with eyes? They turned out to be what is called glassfish. Pretty good tasting, though, even if they are *whole*.

I also mentioned table manners in the "Tips" section; even the most refined people will likely pack a whole unshelled shrimp in their mouth—head and all. They will chew, spit a shell, chew more then spit out an antenna or eye, chew more and spit again into their plate. Chewing and spitting is a common sight.

Belching loudly is okay too and goes without an, "Excuse me," or even a notice from anyone around.

Night Markets are something you must experience if you go to Taiwan and China. These flea markets are set up in back-ally narrow streets or side streets, which will close to traffic at night. They sell everything you can think of, including some interesting food products.

The smells of some of the items that are being cooked for consumption on the street can get fairly nasty and I have no idea what some of this food is derived from. Some smells can gag a maggot. Rotted garbage during a New York City Sanitation Workers strike in mid August may smell a little better than some of this street fare, especially what they call "stinky Tofu."

What is fascinating is to see the market items for the local patron to buy and take home to cook. Things like pig faces; the masks of skin removed from a pig and dozens of them stacked, standing at a reclining angle, on a metal cookie sheet. What they are used for I do not want to know. I don't think they celebrate Halloween. Perhaps they wear them to imitate 'Pig Face,' the character in the movie *The Taipei Chainsaw Massacre*.

Other cookie sheets may be stacked with bloodied brains from what appeared to be monkeys, whole octopus, fish heads, duck tongues neatly stacked in rows, sea creatures looking more like alien life forms and many other things that defy description.

Some of the smells are okay and some are foul and sour as you walk by the busy kiosks selling mystery foods. Since there is no refrigeration for these food items on the street, most of the food trays have a small motor that is mounted above it. A piece of coat-hanger wire is attached horizontally to the motor and ribbons are attached to the ends of the coat hanger wire. As the motor spins, the ribbons shoo the flies off the rather gross-looking food items and pig faces.

Some night markets in the smaller cities in the south of Taipei have even more bizarre things. In Tainan, I saw the chef with a huge yellow, live python trying to kill it by banging its head on a steel pole. This was going to be the "Special of the Day." Mmmm. Mmmm.

In, Kaohsiung, pronounced Gow'- Shung, walking into what looked like a typical U.S. deli, I saw that the glass-fronted refrigerated cases were stocked with prepared trays of unidentified items. I was drawn to a cookie sheet with neatly aligned pieces of what looked like tasty black radiator hose stuffed with rice and something else. I asked my associate, "What is that?"

Searching his mind for the correct translation word he began tapping his chest with his index finger, and then finally said, "How you say . . . artery?"

"Artery! From what?" I asked in amazement.

"Horse."

All I could think was, *Why?* And I didn't ask what it was stuffed with.

The most bizarre was the outdoor food concession in Kenting National Park at the southern-most tip of Taiwan. The Taiwanese equate this to our Yellowstone National Park. It's nice, but not even close to Yellowstone. The only animals I was aware of were various birds and some poisonous snakes that I was told were released by the Japanese near the end of World

War II. Supposedly, they were being bred as weapons for jungle fighting. This is a location where it is so humid the stiff breeze from the ocean just blows the sweat off of you and onto the person standing behind you.

A wide variety of food is offered as is at night markets but a lot more 'regional' foods were displayed at Kenting. You know, kind of like grits, biscuits and gravy you can get in the Southern U.S., only weirder.

The strangest was the vendor who had three charcoal hibachis set up to custom-grill his unusual fare. As I looked at his table, memories of the old cartoons I watched as a kid came to mind. Perhaps you remember when cartoons depicted a dead or knocked-out bird with an "X" or cross in the eyes and its head cocked to one side? The tray full of various size, completely plucked birds, heads tilted limply to one side and eyes closed and looking like those cartoon birds were stacked on the usual metal cookie sheets.

The birds were 'whole,' not gutted, and ranged from sparrow-size to crow-size and all sizes in between. Each bird had a wooden skewer up its bottom so it could be easily placed on the hibachi, grilled and rotated, then handed to the customer so it could be eaten right off the stick as the patron walked around.

I was told this is an illegal practice of netting songbirds in flight and selling them in this manner. We were in a National Park and most likely any law enforcement officer would bend the rules for a free barbequed, naturally stuffed, crow. The same as government officials everywhere, I guess. Give them a free blue jay once in a while and they'll look the other way.

Crow. Bet it tastes just like—bald eagle.

***

Karaoke in most of Asia is extremely popular. As I rode around the cities I saw what I thought were broadcast centers for a station called KTV. I soon discovered it stands for Karaoke Television.

We're not talking a bar and a little stage. We're talking a huge building with various size private rooms that can cater to parties of a few to fifty or more. You can purchase drinks, snacks and be served by your personal wait staff.

You can also purchase pindo nuts. They are from a type of palm tree and they are chewed to give you an energy spike. I am not sure if it is caffeine or what but they taste awful. I guess if you chew tobacco you may like it, but one chomp and I spit it out.

Fortunately, it is acceptable to spit.

All the electronics, sound systems and video equipment is all top notch and there are thousands of songs in Chinese but some really crappy old ones in English. Still, it is a lot of fun.

***

Taiwan Tips rule number one is 'Watch Your Step' and I mean this literally.

Sidewalks are almost never a flat, uniform walking surface. They can have varying elevations, unintended steps, holes or other traps for the unsuspecting Westerner to trip over or fall into. The comment about not being in Kansas anymore needs to be recognized. You are not going to be able sue anyone because you tripped on a raised section of sidewalk, or slipped on some unidentifiable substance and skinned you toes and your nose.

Parked motorbikes cover many sidewalks completely so you will need to take your life into your hands and walk in the street, sometimes for a block or more, to get around them. There seems to be no common sense to protect the pedestrian from injury.

The same is true in building construction techniques. Scaffolding, on the outer side of buildings under construction or repair, may still be made from bamboo for buildings fewer than twenty floors. Although very strong, it is only tied together with rope and I have seen some pretty old, rotted rope tying cross-members together.

Never walk under it. Things are dropped from above often and pedestrians are injured regularly and killed occasionally.

The inside of buildings is another place to watch your step. Most doorway thresholds are raised two or three inches so you need to step over them or trip over them or jam your toes back into your heels.

My first experience with this type of threshold was in the hotel room on my very first night in Taiwan. I got up in the middle of the night and slammed my delicate toes into the threshold's raised trap. I thought I surely had broken a few of my lower digits. I didn't, but I did have a very colorful red and purple bruise across the top my foot behind my toes.

Bathrooms are the worst, especially the ones in hotels or public buildings that cater mostly to locals. It seems that many Taiwanese men do no use the tub to take a shower. They will just grab the hand-held showerhead and douse themselves in the middle of the bathroom floor. For this reason there is always a drain in the floor and I assume it gets blocked occasionally. So to keep the water in the bathroom, and to damage Yankee Boy's toes, the thresholds are raised two or three inches for this reason.

Another deadly stupid prank was one hotel's floor-mounted doorstopper that kept the shower door from hitting the toilet and breaking the glass. Great planning and design here. Why would anyone put it in front of the toilet in the middle of the floor? This is another dangerous foot killer when you forget to look down or enter the bathroom half asleep during the night. Even one of my Taiwanese associates had some foot damage during the middle of the night and commented on how stupid the placement was.

"But why high thresholds in office buildings?" I asked. I was told in case of a typhoon. But we were on the third floor at the time. Go figure. If rain blows in the windows it will be trapped inside.

Because it is uncomfortable wearing steel-toed shoes to bed, I now only stay at hotels that cater primarily to Westerners. Thresholds at these hotels are flat.

***

Public restrooms can be a unique experience. Usually, in Taipei, or other major cities, places that are more modern or cater to Western business people have modernized the restroom facilities.

But what is the *experience* you ask?

Many restrooms in suburban areas do not have standard toilets; at least as we know them. Some, and mostly in outlying regions or older parts of cities, have a low porcelain fixture that essentially surrounds a hole on the floor. Visualize an elongated hole, surrounded by the perhaps one inch high porcelain rim with a half rounded raised cup-like shield in the front. This is designed so, as you are squatting over the hole, any forward spray of urine will not hit the floor in front of you. It will deflect down into the hole. This device requires quite the balancing act since you squat over it. Fortunately, I have avoided the use of this devious device.

The mental visual is a real prank. There is nothing to hold on to. And that forward shield? Really not needed. Because if you drop your pants and your clothing is around your ankles, it will be blocking the spray anyway unless you strip completely from the waist down. Not a pretty sight.

In parks and roadside areas you may need to fill a bucket with water for a final flush or should I say rinsing the fixture and surrounding area. Don't worry, buckets are usually provided for free.

Men have it a little easier, at least partly. Urinals are sometimes nothing more than what looks like a long cattle trough, but at least we guys can stand.

The final restroom prank is where to wash you hands. You will usually look around and note there is no sink in the John. Great, now what?

As you push through the semi-see-through privacy curtain, beads or sometimes nothing at all, you may notice a sink somewhere outside the restroom. Whether the sink is inside or outside the restroom, there usually will not be any towels. So just shake 'em off and be happy you didn't fall over at the hole while squatting and performing that strategic balancing act.

***

One experience you really do not want to miss is to tour one of the big Buddhist temples in Tainan and the huge, beautiful Buddhist monastery in Nantou. I'm serious here.

At the huge Tucheng Luer Men Sain Mu Temple in Tainan, you will be amazed by the hand-carved backdrops on the vast walls. Meticulously carved designs, symbols and figures of gods, dragons and other creatures in each of the various partition-walls are mesmerizing. Everything is painted red, gold and black in deep contrast. Carved statuary of Buddha in different stages of his life, and other religious figures seem to follow your moves with their eyes as you gawk in amazement at the handcrafted skills of master carvers. The smell of incense permeates the air and it is part of the prayer ritual and adds to your senses while absorbing the experience.

On another visit one of my Taiwan associates made an appointment for me to get a private VIP tour of the Chung Tai Chan Monastery in Nantou, Taiwan. She told the Buddhist nun who sets up the tours that I was a big shot American businessman who was gaining an interest in Buddhism.

Not true, but the tour was most fascinating, interesting and enlightening. I was surprised she lied to the nun since she is a devout Buddhist. I guess since Buddhists don't need to confess their sins to anyone, it's okay.

The place was amazing and extremely beautiful. It was overwhelming for a humble little thirty-seven stories, at a cost of 3.6 billion NT Dollars, (about $110,000,000.00 U.S. dollars at the time). The monastery houses a thousand Buddhist monks and nuns and several hundred lay people.

Stone statues, some sixty-feet tall, made from granite and marble from around the globe and some made from gold were everywhere. The building was a melding of both Eastern and Western design. Very unique and very beautiful.

One thing that seems to stand out to us Americans is the use of the Swastika in the décor of Buddhist temples. There were many of them incorporated into the various structures, especially in the most intricate carvings and tapestries. Depending upon who you ask, its meaning is a symbol of peace, or life, or good-luck. It is interesting how one person in history can take a symbol that is three thousand years old, that signifies good things, then bastardize it into a symbol of hate.

Looking up the word I found the definition stated; "SWASTIKA is derived from the Sanskrit word: SVASTIKAH, which means 'being fortunate'."

**

Politically, Mainland China considers Taiwan a province of the Peoples Republic of China, the PRC. Taiwan considers itself independent, which it is. It has its own president and parliamentary form of government and it is not a Communist country.

However, when an election is impending, China will rattle a few sabers to try to frighten the voters into electing candidates 'friendly' to the PRC.

The first time I went to Taiwan even the U.S. news was reporting China's muscle flexing and threats due to the upcoming election. The Chinese Navy was practicing missile launches in the Straights of Taiwan during that early October so there was definitely a lot of tension in the air.

Not too concerned, but certainly aware there could be a situation, I arrived at CKS Airport late in the afternoon of October 9th and was driven to my hotel in Taipei.

Since I only slept a few hours on the plane I thought I would be able to go to bed around ten or eleven that night and get up the next morning, slipping successfully into the local time zone, which is thirteen hours ahead of Eastern Standard Time from where I had left. No such luck.

I tossed and turned on the rock-hard bed and realized I was not going to sleep. I turned on the TV and scanned the channels and settled on watching BBC news for a while until I was totally bored, but still wide awake.

Get some fresh air was my thought.

I got dressed and went downstairs to take a walk. When I exited the hotel I turned to the right and began my brisk walk. Since it was around 2:00 AM I didn't think much about the lack of activity on the streets. A motorbike would occasionally wiz by but no cars. No cars? I thought this was a little unusual.

Just walking straight on this main drag, about seven or eight blocks later I heard a cacophony of rumbling noise from behind me. I turned and saw that several blocks away the noise was being caused by some large vehicles coming my way. Was it large trucks?

Since it was a little unnerving not seeing many people and almost no traffic, I thought it best to turn around and head back to the hotel.

The rumbling noise got louder as the gap was being closed between the source of the racket and me but I could only see headlights approaching.

Stopping dead in my tracks, I finally saw what was approaching; China had invaded Taiwan!

Personnel carriers, Jeeps with machine guns mounted in the back, military vehicles carrying missile launchers, antiaircraft cannons and other olive-drab and camo-colored military trucks were passing as I stood there in a bit of a state of shock. Then came the tanks clanking and lumbering down the street with their big guns pointing straight ahead.

Shit! This was bad.

As I high-tailed it back to the hotel more military vehicles were coming toward me, then continuing down this main avenue.

Finally entering my hotel I went to the desk clerk and asked if he was aware of the invasion. He now appeared not to understand English, although he had earlier.

I guessed the cowardly son of a bitch was already kissing up to the conquerors. He must have thought that speaking English to an American was going to be a crime to the Communist Chinese. He finally said, "Sorry sir, what you mean?"

"What do you mean, what do I mean?! Look outside man! What the hell do you call that?" I shouted at him.

"That Taiwan Army," he said with a smile.

This guy was pissing me off. "So where are they going?" I asked, thinking now that if these were Taiwan's vehicles they were probably locating them where there would be a battle at the other end of town, or maybe at the airport or at the big Karaoke TV (KTV) building.

"They go to president's house—like your White House."

Now I was baffled—a battle at the Taiwan White House equivalent? Something just didn't fit here so I simply said, "Explain."

After the clerk suffered through an explanation I felt like the second character in the movie *Dumb and Dumber.*

Even though it felt I had arrived today, October 9th, it was already past midnight and the next day was at hand. I was not aware that October 10th was what the Taiwanese people called Double Ten or 10/10 Day, their Independence Day. The desk clerk explained that it was a national holiday tomorrow, or actually later today, and the military vehicles were to be staged for a celebration parade to begin at the presidential residence the next morning.

Now talk about feeling like an idiot.

Chinese invasion, indeed—who knew?

***

One of the initial requirements I mentioned is your need to be thick skinned. One contributing reason for this is due to some of the things you will endure with most of the Asian cultures. It may or may not be that anyone is intentionally being rude to you but many times it is a language thing.

For example: Let's say you have not been to the Asian country for quite a few months and over the last holidays, a few weeks ago, you pigged out as usual and put on a few extra kilos of blubber.

Here in the U.S. your friends will tell you, "Hey, you're looking good, mighty-man," then tell others, "Wow, it looks like he's stocking up for the great famine," the two-faced bastards.

But many of the various Asian languages don't allow for twenty ways from Monday to describe things, so the translations will be more like, "Hello. Good to see you; you got fat."

Or, here is a nice one: "How come your hair is white but eyebrows black. You look funny."

I chuckle at the common Asian consensus that all of us American white guys with gray hair all look alike. I have been told I look like Newt Gingrich, Bill Clinton and George Bush. And once, when I decided to grow a beard for a while, I found myself in a tiny restaurant signing autographs as Kenny Rogers for the string bean snapper girls.

The time I was told I got fat had an added insult. A few days later, my Taiwanese associate, ninety-pound Suzy, said we were going to fly to our factory in Tainan instead of driving. *Great*, I thought. A half-hour flight instead of a three to four hour drive was going to be easier.

She then informed me, "I get you ticket on fat airline."

Okay, Suzy, be a bitch and rub it in, I was thinking. But she never cracked a smile or made any further comment, so I just assumed this was a normal way to treat a semi fat-ass from the U.S.

We arrived at Taipei City Airport. She parked the car and we walked into the terminal building.

Moments later I saw we were approaching a ticket counter with a large sign behind the agent with the letters FAT. I could not believe that Suzy had arranged this super, 'skinny bitch prank' at the airport.

I wanted to say to her, "Did you know your ass looks like two flat little pancakes with a couple of bones clacking together?" but I didn't because she would probably just play dumb and say, "What is pancakes?"

So I said nothing and made believe I didn't notice this obvious prank.

However, as I received my boarding pass, I read FAT printed on the background of the ticket. This prank was out of control now.

We passed through security and got to the assigned gate. As I looked out to the tarmac I saw that on the side of one of the planes was the word FAT on the tail . . . and on the side of the plane it read, "FAR-EASTERN AIR TRANSPORT."

The sneaky bastards.

***

There is one important item I should mention. Taiwan is a volcanic island so there is a great deal of seismic activity occurring every day. There are over two thousand earthquakes a year that occur in its shifting geology.

Fortunately, most are just tremors and many occurring unnoticed in remote areas. But occasionally there are some really huge ones.

In September of 1999 a magnitude 7.7 quake in central Taiwan, near Nantou took the lives of more than 2400 people and injured thousands more. The land shifted and pushed up a vertical offset that measured more than nine meters, almost thirty feet, causing an entire mountain to slide into the valley below and disappear forever. Over the next several weeks there were a total of more than 10,000 aftershocks; four were greater than magnitude 6.5 continued to shake the island.

I was there about a month after the earthquake and saw the damage in Taipei, especially in some of the older sections of the city, which was about a hundred miles from the epicenter.

Usually there are instructions in hotel rooms in case of an earthquake. They are more humorous than instructional. Statements like, "Do not fall out window." instead of, "Stay away from windows," make me laugh and not take it seriously.

So I suggest you search it on the Internet for the correct and complete information about earthquake preparations and responses.

***

Mainland China is the same in many ways and in some ways worse. Traffic is still out of control but it is much worse by adding bicycles, rickshaws and hoards of pedestrians all going in different directions at the same time with no regard to lanes, rules or common sense. It is truly a wonder that China's population is so high. Perhaps it is the government's method of population control. Insane and dangerous is an understatement.

Even though we occasionally hear about some human rights atrocities in China, we still tend to forget it is still a Communist country.

Factories in China have barracks-like buildings attached, or on the property to house the workers. Imagine if in your current job you say good-bye to your fellow workers, but then had to walk with them to your rooms a hundred feet away. Later, you will see them in the mess hall for dinner. Because some of your fellow workers are on kitchen duty this month they get to leave a little earlier to prepare meals for you and several hundred other workers.

On laundry day your undies will be hanging from the balcony and flapping in the hot sticky breeze outside of your third floor, one room residence in which you, your wife, who is also employed at the factory, and child share with your and/or her parents.

At this time there is not much of a middle class in China. However, statistics now show that there are almost three hundred million buyers of high-end luxury electronics items and autos. That is almost the population of the United States, of which only about twenty-five percent are considered high-end buyers. So as a market potential China is a huge business opportunity for all types of products.

The other billion-plus people are striving for better opportunities, like perhaps changing jobs because they give them nicer company logo shirts. Or, they may be saving their money for a new bicycle but will most likely never be able to buy a car or even own a motorbike.

Things have improved for the average worker though. Companies are offering more leisure time and a pittance of higher wages. There are a few more holidays and some companies have even reduced the number of work-hours.

As this happens, the cost per employee rises, not that they see much, if anything, in their meager stipend. A factory that is not cranking out their line of lead-paint lipsticks and still has people to feed and house at fixed expenses has to raise prices, hence increasing costs to U.S. consumers.

Some foreign companies have been unionized. To my understanding, no domestic companies have union — only some foreign ones.

A unionized strike in China is different than in the US. There, the workers will take over the building, then take management hostage and perhaps beat or torture them until their demands are met. The police pretty much allow them to riot outside the factory and work out the details for themselves inside. There are no scabs here.

Hong Kong is a different story. It has its own currency and has remained fairly autonomous from many of the Mainland's business methods since the Chinese government took it over from the British in 1997. It remains more Westernized.

Vietnam and India are a couple of the new discount labor centers because their people now work more hours per week and more days per year than the Chinese. Did you know there are more English-speaking people in India that in the US? (True fact from the inside of a Snapple cap.)

There are a number of American companies that have set up shop in China. Since the government owns everything it could be disastrous if there ever becomes a serious political problem between the U.S. and China, or China and Taiwan. Huge companies could potentially go out of business and Wal-Mart inventory would dry up in a week.

In 1997, when Hong Kong reverted back to China from Great Britain, I thought for sure Hong Kong businesses would crash and burn due to the notorious ability for China's local players to keep corruption on the cutting edge. Fortunately, the government put the clamp on it so to keep the Hong Kong economic region affluent and running fairly well. Hong Kong Island still has its own currency and many outsiders don't relate it to Mainland China, as they should. It is governed independently but I believe it may be a bit of a farce. That's only my opinion, however.

Nothing is ever perfect, and Hong Kong still thrives, so I assume it's not too bad, or as bad as elsewhere in the country.

***

By now you know about the dangers for pedestrians in the Asian streets. Not to be omitted, here is an important warning about Japan.

When we were kids we were told to look both ways before crossing the street. As you got older you learned to automatically look to your left first because that is where the car that will hit you will come from the quickest. So the usual procedure is to look left, you don't see anything, then step into the street and look to your right for traffic coming the opposite way. Right?

In Japan, as in England, Australia and some other countries, the vehicles drive on the left side of the road. This is a difficult thing to get used to as an American driver, and it is also difficult to get used to as a pedestrian.

At first thought, you may not even think how extremely dangerous it is to be a pedestrian as you begin to cross a street not at a traffic light. So as usual, if you look left and do not see anything coming in your direction you will blindly step into the street, casually turning to your right to look for the oncoming traffic on the opposite side of the street. Well surprise, surprise! You just may see a close-up of the grill of a Toyota speeding at you from your right and near the curb. What an unusual hood ornament you will make.

This is a hard habit to overcome until that one time when this happens and your adrenalin rush causes you to do a near back flip and you land on your backside realizing you just had a near-death experience.

Despite the left handed driving anomaly I found Japan a very interesting place to visit. It is a blend of modern, cutting-edge technologies and ancient traditions. Bridges, roadways, high-speed bullet trains are technical marvels.

And what about Kansai Airport that was built in Osaka Bay on an island that was created from scratch? Sounds easy. Just dump a few rocks in the water that is sixty feet deep, three miles from shore and make an island two and a half miles long and four thousand feet wide . . . an amazing feat—even if it is currently sinking.

The first time I flew into Osaka's Kansai I was impressed by its magnificence. Kansai has one of the most beautiful terminal buildings I have ever seen. Italian architect Renzo Piano designed it and it is noted as the most appealing airport terminal in the world.

The train, then bus ride to Kobe, showed the density of population in this crowded country. As I approached the city, it appeared to be larger than New York .

Once I arrived in Kobe I checked into my hotel. It was called the Sannomiya Terminal Hotel.

Now, I don't know how *you* feel staying at a hotel called "Terminal," but I began to think of a Japanese version Hitchcock's *Psycho*.

For 19,000.00 yen per day, about $190.00 U.S. at the time, the hotel room was not much bigger than a six-by-nine cell in San Quentin Prison. (Not that I would know.) The bed was smaller than a standard U.S. twin bed and unless I slept in a fetal position my feet would hang over the bed touching the desk. But happily, the bed was not a hard as Taiwan and China beds.

The bathroom was interesting to say the least. Standing in the middle I could touch opposite walls, in any direction, without fully extending my arms. The sink was directly against the toilet on the right side and actually hung into the tiny tub / shower on the left. If you decided to take a bath, you would need to sit in the tub with your knees to your chest to fit. There was barely room to turn around in the room.

The toilet was interesting. There were two buttons on the tank top: one white, one red. Looking at the location of the buttons it would be difficult, if not impossible, to press them if you were sitting on the bowl. So obviously, they were meant to be pressed while standing in front of the commode. Wouldn't you agree?

I pressed the white one first and magically a little white plastic arm swung out from the inside rim of the bowl to its center. This was starting to remind me of an old joke that I will not go into here. I then pressed the red button and a geyser of fairly hot water shot out of the little arm right into my face.

I let go of the button and as I pulled my face back out of the firing line, the water continued to shoot up, now hitting the ceiling then raining down on me and the rest of the tiny room. I could have used one of those high entrance-thresholds here, but no such luck.

I leaned around the geyser and hit the red button again, finally ending the towering spray. I hit the white button again and the arm retracted.

That wonderful Japanese engineering of a toilet – bidet combo should have included a towel and a change of clothes, which were then required.

So rule number one for Japan is don't push the buttons unless you are sitting—if you can reach them.

***

In my opinion, Japanese food is far better than Chinese food, or at least I like it better. Much is the same as you would get here in American Japanese restaurants. Sure, there are some strange things, but they just don't come off as nasty and I don't seem to need the old Pepto Bismol.

Once, I was in Japan with an associate from the U.S., Gary, whose wife is Japanese and his in-laws still lived there. He spoke a little Japanese and knew his way around pretty well . . . except maybe for the rail system, but more on that later.

We had visited a potentially large customer in Hamamatsu. When we were finished he asked me if I liked Ramon.

"Noodles?" I asked.

He said, "Yep. I know the best place in Japan."

He explained how in Japan they pride themselves on never cleaning pots where certain types of foods are prepared. They allow a crust of old broths to build layers of what is believed to be a flavor-enhancing scum. It kind of looks like old, yellowing, calcified water pipes encrusted with minerals that have leached out from a leak for a century, while buried under the streets of New York City. Nice visual here.

These pots are never emptied and are simmered continuously. They just add liquid and ingredients as necessary, so theoretically, remnants of the very first Ramon cooked in that pot decades ago were still there.

As we sat on the little counter stools I looked around and noted the large encrusted pots. Some had layers up to between two and three inches thick. Others were encrusted thinly in spots where it appeared the crust had broken off and was on the mend with new growth appearing.

I noticed the condiment basket. It too had never been cleaned. The wicker weave had crusts of its own; I couldn't guess what they were. The city soot was also layered on the flattop shakers of salt, black and red pepper and other unidentifiable seasonings.

The floor was ancient, unfinished concrete with a trough about a foot wide in its center, which ran out to the street. I later saw the purpose for this; it was to throw unconsumed broth of Ramon and also to dump the rinse water from the serving bowls. Yes, I said rinse, not wash.

The few bits of noodle would eventually make it to the street and would be consumed by birds or an occasional stray dog or cat.

The Ramon noodles were hand made in this little shop by a man that looked older than dirt and not much cleaner. Everything looked filthy but it smelled great.

The Ramon selections were available with of chicken, pork, beef, all types of veggies, crab, shrimp, scallops and fish chunks, or any combination of the choices.

I ordered the shrimp and crab combo. The thickly crusted pots did their job and as I shook a little hot red pepper and soot into my broth my appetite raged. It was amazingly good.

This process of never ending pots of food was again used in a restaurant in Nagoya.

The region is famous for a seasonal dish called Hamo Shabu. This is similar to Shabu Shabu, which is a beef dish that is cooked fondue style in a never-ending, heavily encrusted pot.

Hamo Shabu, however, is made with a stock from a fish called Hamo. It is also known as a pike eel or dagger tooth conger. It is one ugly snake-like creature with teeth that are in rows like a freshwater pike. But in the broth, cooked properly, it is one delicious meal.

Gary's father-in-law was with an independent rep firm in Japan. He was able gain access for me to the engineering department of a division of Sony and did most of the interpreting for me at the meeting. Since it was late in the day, when we finished our meetings, he took us to a restaurant famous for Hamo Shabu.

There were four of us: Gary, his father-in-law, his business partner, and me. We removed our shoes and were shown into a private, but fairly large, dining room where a large, dark, hardwood table sat low to the floor in the center of the ornate room. It probably could have seated at least twenty people but it was set up for just the four of us.

Two large pots simmered at each end of the table and two waitresses dressed in kimonos stood at attention bowing their heads as we were seated on the cushioned floor. Round, clear-glass, globe-like pitchers, with a blown ice pockets were brought to the table. These were filled with sweet, clear sake, which was ice cold.

In the U.S. I had always had sake warm and thought that was the Japanese way. But no, I was being introduced to something with a totally different flavor. This was simply Japanese Kool-Aid, and that can be dangerous.

Surprisingly, the tiny little sake glasses we use in U.S. Japanese restaurants were replaced with a four-ounce rocks glass.

Next came platters of raw fish squares, mushrooms, onions, clear noodle and other local vegetables. The waitresses placed enough for four servings into the simmering pots and cooked each item to its individual perfection.

For the next several hours we talked and ate and I discovered a very interesting Japanese technology; the sake glasses were like the never-ending Shabu pots—they never emptied. I knew I just drank some but when I turned to look at my glass again it was full. Amazing, these Japanese!

Finally, after a pound or two of ragged-toothed slippery eel, veggies and I guess a gallon of sake, we were ready to leave.

I looked around for my briefcase and didn't see it. What I did see was what I thought was Gary's large suitcase. Oddly, it was not the same tan color I remembered him carrying in. This was black, the same color as my briefcase.

"Gary. Is that your bag?" I asked.

Gary laughed. He was red-faced. He must have had too much sake to drink. But not me, I was straight as an arrow. "No, man. That's your briefcase."

Couldn't be. That thing was the size of a trunk by that point. Jesus, it got even bigger since I first looked at it. What the hell was wrong with my eyes? Sake sight, I guess.

I started thinking, *What if everything looks huge?* Hey, now I can't wait to get back to my hotel room! I think they had a full-length mirror.

At my hotel when I sat on my bed and started to remove my shoes, it finally hit me that I was, as they say in Japanese . . . shit-faced san.

I popped off one shoe and tossed it on the floor. I had just slipped the other off when some movement caught my attention out of the corner of my eye. I turned my head toward the wall to my right and again saw another quick movement.

I stared at the area, a little bleary-eyed and again, movement. Now I saw what it was. My God, it was a cockroach the size of a good Cuban cigar.

In sake slow motion I raised the shoe and began to attempt to aim my wingtip at the Godzilla-Roach. Suddenly, it streaked down the wall and under my bed.

Screw it! I was in no condition for a hunting expedition. I crawled under the covers, got into a fetal position and went to sleep.

The following morning while I was getting dressed for the day I caught the movement again. This time it was on the floor, along the edge of the wall, heading for the door. However, it must have been the younger brother of the one from last night because this one was only half the size of a Cuban cigar. Still pretty damned big.

With wingtip in hand, held by the toe, I dived at the now growling, snarling monster and whacked it a shot with the heel of the shoe. It seemed to turn toward me and say, "Is that all you got, round eyes?"

The next shot slowed it down a bit more and it now looked like a soldier crawling to his foxhole with his left arm injured. It dragged itself toward the door, pulling with its right legs, determined to defeat me. But this was going to be this bastard's Hiroshima.

Whack! Now it ceased all forward motion but was still alive; I could see it was still breathing. It may have been trying to play possum, waiting for me to turn my back on it, then attack my feet, or worse, escape out the door and return while I was sleeping during the night and do God knows what.

But no, I watched as his growling ceased, breathing slowed and eyes began to glaze over. The monster was on its way out.

Even though this may or may not have been the sake-sized one I saw last night, it was still the biggest roach I had ever seen. I had to show Gary this thing or he would never believe me. I found an envelope in the desk drawer so I scraped the big bug into it and folded the flap without sealing it—I surely didn't want to lick that envelope. I then put it in my briefcase.

Later that morning Gary and I were in the lobby of Mitsubishi where we had a meeting scheduled. Opening my briefcase I said to Gary, "You've got to see this."

However, as I opened the bag a foul odor reached my nostrils and I saw the envelope was very wet—and flat.

I peeked inside; Godzilla-Roach was even larger because it was flatter than splat.

"Jesus, Bob, what's that stink?" Gary asked with his face all scrunched up in reaction to the smell.

I showed him and said, "What in Hell am I going to do with it now? I can't just go up and ask the receptionist to put this stinking thing in the wastebasket."

Fortunately, there were some large potted plants in the lobby. So, while Gary distracted the receptionist I mailed the letter to the base of a fern and ficus pot.

Ding-dong, the roach is dead.

***

Trains and subway heavily dominate transportation system in Japan. As a visitor you can purchase a rail pass for a selected number of days and travel the entire country. These rail passes are not cheap, however. I don't recall the exact amount but it was around three hundred dollars for only two or three days. This fee did not include subway trains. That was a pay-as-you-go fare system and the fee was based on your total distance to the destination. Again, this was not cheap either.

When you buy a ticket for a particular stop you must be able to recognize the kanji, or Japanese symbol, for the stop's location.

I studied the kanji and determined it looked like a little house with a cat's tail sticking out of the upstairs window. As the subway train would pull into the station, the little houses all started to look alike: Tail out the left window, the right, two tails, tail out the correct window but not curled enough. Anyway, I passed my station by miles.

Not being able to speak Japanese and not having Gary with me to make use his limited Japanese, I was using hand signals and making faces at a subway employee and pointing to my ticket stub as to where I needed to go. He finally understood and put up six fingers and pointed toward the direction I had just come from, which I assumed meant six stops back.

I then had to go up an eight-story escalator, and another three long flights of stairs to purchase another ticket, go back down to the platform and get off on the sixth stop, which was the correct little house and cat's tail symbol. Oh, and did I mention I was moving to another hotel and dragging around all of my luggage for this excursion? Plenty of exercise that day.

Traveling by auto is also expensive. Gary's father-in-law drove us about twenty miles on a toll road and the fee was thirty thousand yen, about thirty dollars.

Most all of us guys have liked trains since we were kids and the Japanese trains are the slickest around. They look like rocket ships and the Bullet Trains *are* like rocket ships.

I was on the Bullet from downtown Tokyo to Narita Airport and how impressive it was. It reaches top speed of 277 MPH and as you are racing along, the tea plantations and any structures close to the rails are nothing more than a blur.

The downside is that the train takes a long time to come to a stop as it begins its deceleration process slowly so passengers are not suddenly slammed to the forward walls of the cars. This increases the average time for short runs by a considerable margin and decreases the average speed to around 160 MPH. That's still not too shabby.

I like Japan. Since I am a keeper of Japanese koi and have a large pond in my backyard, some day I will visit just for fun and go to the areas where the "Living Jewels," as they are called, are raised.

Chapter 16

Time Zones

We have all heard of *Jet Lag*. Or, as one of my Taiwanese associates calls it, "Jet Leg." Time differences between U.S. cities, with the exception of Alaska and Hawaii, are no more than a three-hour difference from coast to coast. But it seems that some people have difficulty coping with the time differences, some even at only an hour.

At my office I marvel at the people who will complain about how screwed up they are because of the one hour weekend time variance due to daylight savings time changes. I want to slap them sideways and say, "Get over it fool! You had all day Sunday to adjust." As you can tell, it annoys me how spoiled and whiney some people are. We are in a world of whiney wussies and it is getting worse.

One to three hours is easy for anyone to deal with; it just takes a little planning. Since I travel coast-to-coast most often

I developed a routine that works best for me. Understand that I begin my trips from the East Coast and I believe it is easier from east to west than those from west to east.

Normally I book the very first morning flight out to my destination, usually between 6:00 AM and 8:00 AM. This is good for few reasons.

First, since you are up and out before the crack of dawn there will usually be no rush hour traffic. Hence, you will cruise to the airport without worrying about a minor accident causing a monumental traffic jam and you miss your flight.

Secondly, the airport will be crowded, but not as bad as usual. Seldom will it be crowded to the point where the lines wrap around the building. So you will usually breeze through check-in and security and can have breakfast at the airport and plenty of time to board your flight. Or, if you are able to join an airline's club lounge you can get coffee, juice, light food or a Bloody Mary for breakfast for free. Well, not exactly for free; the membership fees are usually two to three hundred dollars per year. But believe me, it is well worth it, when you are delayed for several hours and can sit in a comfy chair, use an office cubicle to conduct business, get free wireless networking and use of copiers, fax, and other office machines. There is usually a TV room and most times there are no kids running around, yelling and making you psychotic.

Next point is booking the first plane out. This is truly important because your plane will most always have been there since the night before. You won't be waiting for your plane to arrive from another city, perhaps late due to weather, mechanical or other issues since it is there already.

Once you get comfortable and have your noise cancelling head phones on and your inflatable pillow in place, you can make up the few hours of lost sleep because of getting up at three-thirty while you are on your way. Sleeping also magically makes your trip shorter, like my best ever flight to Saint Louis, unless, of course, you are dreaming about flying to China, then it may feel longer. Then, as you prepare to land in say, Los

Angeles, you are fairly rested and it is usually not past noon at your destination. Since you have nothing scheduled except a dinner appointment you can go have lunch, check into your hotel a bit early and prepare everything for the rest of your trip, check your e-mails and relax for the afternoon. Try not to take a nap, however. You want to be tired in the evening so you can go to sleep your regular time. Then, tomorrow you will be on schedule as if you were at home.

Do the same thing on your return trip; get the first flight out for the same reasons. This time try not to sleep on the plane, or sleep only for perhaps an hour. By doing that you will be fairly tired and will be able to go to sleep your regular time in your home time zone.

This works whether you are beginning or ending your trip from either coast. If you are beginning from the West Coast you will not have gotten enough sleep so you can eat an early dinner, relax in your room and get to sleep the time you would at home and be ready to slay the dragon the next day.

Beyond three hours you will need to get a routine that works for you. Don't listen to any of the old wives tales about cardboard in your shoes or pennies in your underwear. Besides, the pennies will have to come out at security and that will be embarrassing if they have slipped into some bodily crevasse.

I have settled on a routine that works for me on Asian trips. Since Taiwan, China and Japan are mostly thirteen hours time difference during Eastern Standard Time and twelve during Daylight Time I call that "upside-down" time. Middle of the day home is middle of the night there. As noted previously, it surely can be hard to adjust.

At first I thought it would be better to spend a couple of days on the West Coast, then leave for Asia because technically it is closer. And after all, it does cut about six hours off the trip. But that turned out to be fuzzy logic because the West Coast is fifteen or sixteen hours time difference. That made it even worse. So, now I usually bite the bullet and leave as I would normally to the West Coast, at first flight out, and get to L.A. just before noon local time.

The five o' clock EVA Air flight to Taipei is my choice. With this schedule I have a time buffer in case the L.A. arrival is late for any reason and I will still have time for a meal at the airport prior to the long leg of the trip. If you leave on a Monday, this flight will get into Taipei around 10:00 PM on Wednesday due to your crossing of the International Date Line. This gets me to my hotel around midnight and ready for a good night's sleep and on schedule for the remainder of the trip.

The rough part is the return trip to the U.S. The return flight is around 6:00 PM, usually on a Saturday. After twelve or thirteen hours of flying you get to Los Angeles three hours before you left Taipei, the same day. Now that will really tweak your wheels.

The first few times I returned from that trip it would take me nearly three weeks to get back on track. I would find myself unable to stay awake by three in the afternoon so I would need to go to sleep. Then, I would be up at three in the morning and at the office by four, only to repeat the previous day by the afternoon. Ah, but now I have a method.

Since the company owns a townhouse in Las Vegas, instead of returning to Newark after arriving in L.A., I take an hour flight to Vegas. By the time I get there it is local dinnertime, so I'll get a light meal, go back to the house and crash by around 7:30 PM. I will still wake up early in the morning, perhaps around three or four. So off to Denny's I go for some coffee and eggs.

Las Vegas, being a twenty-four hour town, has no shortage of things to do so after breakfast, the casino of my choice is always open. That day I have plenty of things to kill time around town or even some relaxing drives out to the desert. By late afternoon I am dragging, so nap time it is. However, only for about an hour or so then my alarm buzzes me awake. This is a tough one to awake and get the sleepiness out of my body so I take a cool shower and dress for dinner.

Now I force myself to stay awake until ten or eleven. By the next morning I am back in the U.S. mode, getting up at six or seven. I leave first-flight-out the next day and I'm ready again to adapt to my home time zone.

The above works for me. Many people cannot regulate themselves as easily. If you cannot sleep at night you will be worthless in your work the next day. If your stomach is upset and producing acid while you are tossing and turning in your hotel bed you will be miserable that night and worse in the morning. Taking a Benadryl™ or Excedrin PM™ to help you sleep is okay.

Melatonin is a hormone secreted by the pineal gland in humans and allows other body receptors to trigger the body to sleep. It is produced during darkness and it aids your sleep cycles, also known as circadian rhythms. This has been synthesized and is available as a health supplement over the counter here in the U.S. and can be taken to enable you to sleep. It is not a narcotic and should have no side effects as you would have with other sleep aids. But be careful; it is illegal to sell Melatonin in the European Union, New Zealand and perhaps other countries. You can have it, but don't try to sell it.

For me, Excedrin PM™ and Melatonin do not work. Benadryl™ works just fine, but it continues to work for me through most of the next day and I feel hung-over. So my own scheduling does just fine for me.

Chapter 17

The Language Barrier

Do you speak English? Most likely not.

I was on a flight from Las Vegas to Newark recently and was sitting next to a guy from the U.K. who was on his way home from attending a boxing match at Las Vegas' MGM Grand. Now, this man spoke English to his traveling companion and I didn't understand a word he said.

"Elluva foyt lasnoiot, aye?" was about the only thing I got. Translation: "Hell of a fight last night, huh?" The rest I just eventually tuned out because I can understand some Chinese better than that bloke's bloody so-called English gibberish.

Most of us speak 'American,' not English, and like the Chinese language there are many dialects, accents and local terms that you will run into as you travel about the country. For example, for toilet the Britts say loo, we say John, they say filet like fill-it, we say it like fil'-lay, they say foyer as foy-yea and we just say foy-er, we say potato chips, they say crisps – see the differences here?

New York and New Jersey folks will say "you guys or youse guys" whereas the Southeast-to-Texas folks will use the y'awl contraction. The strangest for me is the Pittsburgh to Philadelphia region where many will say you-uns or just yuns. And instead of "mine and yours," it's "my-uns and your-uns." Not a pleasing expression—sounds like urine. That doesn't add to a nice impression.

In parts of the Midwest if you ask for a soda you will get club soda or seltzer. You need to ask for a 'pop' to get a cola or flavored carbonated beverage. In sections of New York they may ask you if you have any 'ideer' what kind of 'soder' you want, Coke or Pepsi. If you ask for a pop you will most likely get a fist in the jaw or a candy on a stick.

In my part of the country a 'regular coffee' is one with milk and two sugars. In the Southeast it is black and in California they will look at you as if you have a third eye and say, "Dude, like is that like a latte or a macchiato? In other places it simply defines only the difference between decaf and non-decaf coffee.

Some regions of the U.S. do not pronounce the letter W in some words.

I was in Southern California working with my rep. He told me we had a meeting with Don Smith at a local company. When Don met us in the lobby I was surprised to see a woman. Maybe it was Don's assistant, I thought at first.

She turned out to be Don, or as her business card read, Dawn Smith.

The 'ahh' instead of 'aw' pronunciation can be annoying unless you are one of those who speak in ahhs. You know, ah-some, ah-full, Dahn, or imitating the sound of a crow: instead of "caw caw" it is "cahh, cahh!" But in parts of New England it's not a crow's call; a cahh is something you drive.

Regional accents and colloquialisms are sometimes difficult, or even downright annoying, until you get used to them. And *yours* will be the same to them so try to develop a neutral accent.

I practiced long and hard, when I was a young salesman, to get rid of the New Jersey accent and now I get people saying, "You don't sound like you're from New Joizey." Which makes me happy I succeeded in creating that neutral accent, if there is such a thing.

Oddly, I don't know anyone in New Jersey who says, "New Joizey." I think they watched too many TV shows of Brooklyn or Queens, New York cops mentioning the perp that skipped over to Joizey. I call it the Kojak Syndrome.

***

Accents or colloquialisms are one thing, but improperly pronounced words are something that makes me crazy—my personal pet peeve. I know a number of people that will mispronounce the same words continuously, like the guy I know that says 'sheddar' cheese instead of cheddar cheese. Even when some of these people are corrected they will say, "Well that's the way *I* say it." Yeah, well you say it wrong, fool! It makes you appear stupid. I need to ask him why he just doesn't say *sheddar sheese.*

There was a radio commercial for a course teaching a better vocabulary that said, "People judge you by the way you speak." Business professionals are not always super smart but if they sound that way they will last a bit longer and may even get by forever. Those who sound dumb from the start can be doomed quickly.

It amazes me how presidents and Congressional politicians cannot pronounce the word "nuclear" properly. When I hear "nuc-u-ler" I want to grab the Pepto Bismol so as not to throw up. It's Nu-cle-ar!

"So let me ax you something." That is another word mispronounced by some. Perhaps it is a symptom of dyslexia. It is possible those people see the word as "aks".

Former New York City mayor Ed Koch once went on a tour of the city schools and discovered teachers were using the erroneous "aks" instead of "ask" and he virtually blew his top. It was a huge news item and a disgraceful report on the New York

City educational system. Whether it did any good or not I am not sure. I'll have to ax someone.

***

Want to know my nominee of the most mispronounced word in the English language? This is the one that really ticks me off. Engineers with degrees in both electrical and electronics, *Double-E's* as they are called, mechanical engineers and even some PHDs are some of the biggest offenders of this verbal faux pas. I hear it everywhere: TV personalities, narrators and do-it-yourself show hosts, home contractors, teachers, professors, politicos and even in a speech of the former First Lady, Laura Bush, this word was used several times incorrectly.

So what is it?

Height.

Yes, 'height' is the most mispronounced word and for some reason it annoys the hell out of me. It seems most people add an *h* to it as if it is *'heighth'*. My guess is that a while ago someone with a speech impediment found it easier to speak about dimensions of width and height by saying width and *heighth*. It easily fits the speech deficiency.

So if you are one of those who add the *h* to the end of the word height, and you don't normally speak like Sylvester the cat, you should take my suggestion and keep the *H* out of it! You will also sound more intelligent. (And not annoy the hell out of me.)

There are several other words that for some reason someone decided to change the pronunciation and all the followers think it is correct. Few will go to a dictionary to question the sudden change in pronunciation, but I will.

Haley's Comet, long 'a' sound has been replaced with Haley, as in Halle Berry.

Himalaya, usually Him-a-'lay-a, is said by some as He-'mohl-ya.

And some words ending in 'e' are made more phony-sophisticated by adding an 'a' inflection at the end. Locally, in

Northwestern New Jersey, the Lenape Indians, pronounced Len-*uh*-pee, became Lenape' [Len-`ahh-pay]. Kobē, Japan has been treated the same way. (Ko-bay)

Pluto was kicked out as a planet but now Uranus, pronounced 'your-anus' [yŏŏ-rā'nəs] for decades changed to Urin-ess, [yŏŏr'ə-nəs]. That pisses me off.

When the U.S. invaded Afghanistan the news intellects all pronounced the capitol city Cobble, as if someone would cobble up a pair of shoes. I only heard two news people pronounce it correctly. The dictionary parses it [**kah**-*bool* or l, k*uh*-**bool.**] And prior to the Iraq invasion, according to the news wizards we were mounting forces in Cutter, not Qtar, which should be pronounced [**kah**-tahr, or k*uh*-**tahr.**] Did these people go to school? And did they ever study geography. Oh, that's right. They don't teach geography any more.

Recently, I just shook my head in disgust when the weather girl spoke of inclement [in-**klem**-*uh*nt] weather, pronouncing it `inkla-mint. I groaned, and then switched to the more intelligent Cartoon Network.

The last straw for me is the silent '*L*' fiasco. A few years ago I started to notice TV talking heads, which really can't talk unless it is written on a teleprompter, would say some words that didn't make sense. If you watch the evening news, many times you will notice they may mispronounce a lot of common words.

The silent '*L*' is being pulled out of its silent past by some and is being pushed it to the verbal forefront with the words calm, palm, almond and salmon. These people will say, "It is kahl-m sitting under pahl-m trees on a bahl-me beach eating al-munds and sal-mon." Oddy, they do not say wahl-k or tahl-k, or writing with chal-k on the blackboard—yet. But some do use a cahlk-ing gun around the bathtub tile.

Almond is an unusual one. The common pronunciation is 'ahh-mund' or the incorrect 'al-mund' but in the regions of northern California where almonds are grown, the people in the business call them 'ammins'. Go figure.

One last observation: Have you ever noticed when you are being polite to perhaps a waiter or other service provider and you are considerate enough to say, "Thank you," to someone and instead of them saying, "You're welcome," or "My pleasure," you will get a, "No problem."

How rude it that? When was it ever a problem and why should it be if they are being paid to do a job or perform a service?

Worse than that is when they just give you a, "Mmm mm" or "Uh-huh" or a really annoying, "You bet." Classy, isn't it? So when your customer, or anyone, says 'thanks' to you, never say that *this* time it wasn't problem and that it *was* truly your pleasure to serve his or her needs. I hope you understand the importance of that.

***

I do believe the way we speak *is* one way in which others will judge you. However, you should never be a philosophunculist (Go look it up) to succeed in your business ventures. Just learn your craft, be honest, personable, and humorous – and try not to mispronounce words whenever professionalism is the order for the day. Dictionaries are made for this purpose, you know.

All right. I'll save you the trouble. A philosophunculist is one who pretends to know more than they do to impress others. Many times those people will be spewing words like "philosophunculist" which they got from *The Book of Impressive Words That No One Uses*.

So if people really *do* judge you on the way you speak and if you impart a confidence in your tone and manner and don't say any dopey things, "Like, duh, dude, hey, lemmie ax you what heighth you need for that part," you will do just fine, even with "yawls" and "you guys" in your repertoire.

So the question we all have to answer is, do we really speak English . . . well?

Chapter 18

Arming the Warrior

Throughout the previous pages there are many suggestions of the weaponry you need to conquer your battles and also the survival methods to keep you up and running for your next joust. I thought it best to sum up this guide by simply listing the things I most often bring with me on business trips.

First item, my suitcase, which is my checked bag. There are some things that are always in my bag even when it is supposed to be empty. Clothes are the variable items, depending on where you are going and how long you will be gone.

Everything to follow remains in my bag, awaiting the next journey into battle.

Toiletry bag contains:
- Hair care items
- Cologne, aftershave

- Dental care items
- Disposable razor (a backup to my electric shaver)
- Deodorant
- Lip balm, cold sore meds
- Band aids
- Antibiotic ointment
- Nail clippers & file
- Collar stays
- Sewing kit
- Oral thermometer
- Sweatband (Trade show booth set up)
- Spoon in a zipper-lock bag
- Eyeglass screwdriver & repair kit (If applicable)
- Larger, but still miniature, slotted/Phillips pocket screwdriver
- Tiny bar of wrapped emergency soap (confiscated from a hotel)
- Small package of laundry detergent (confiscated from a hotel)

Any liquid items in your toiletry bag, shampoo, hairspray, cologne, etc. should be sealed in a zip-bag. The worst thing to leak is shampoo. It not only makes mess in your bag and everything needs to be washed, but as you are rinsing everything a mountain of suds will be billowing out of your hotel room sink.

The pockets and compartments of my bag contain the following collection of items:

- Swiss Army toolkit. This is the king of the Swiss Army knives. It has more than twenty gadgets and over a period of time you will need them all. Or, and equivalent Leatherman tool.
- Electric shaver (Or razor if you prefer)
- Black leather belt.
- Eighteen inch bungee cord
- Extra handkerchiefs
- Pair of cufflinks (If you have any French Cuff shirts and pack one in error)

- Meds (See Chapter 6 for details. Some meds will go in your carry-on.)
- Money clip (Empty. Pack it so it is not a security buzzer.)
- Small folding umbrella (Get a good quality one so when the first time you use it and it blows inside out during a pouring rain, it will recover without you getting drowned. (I know from error experience. Pack in an outside pocket.)
- Nylon windbreaker with hood (For when you are in a short sleeve shirt at Denver airport, late at night, waiting for the hotel shuttle bus, and the temperature drops to a balmy twenty-five degrees, you will be prepared. Pack in an outside pocket.)
- Cloth laundry bag
- A pair of black dress shoes in a cloth tie bag.
- Extra cloth bag(s) for additional shoes
- Liquid shoe polish (Sure paste is better, but you will use this for a fast touch-up of scuffs and scratches or for writing a note on the bathroom mirror to the maid.
- Empty plastic bag (In case you need to need to pack something that can leak or something that is wet or damp).
- Lint roller
- One extra pair of socks and underwear (Or appropriate female attire equivalent)
- Deck of playing cards. (For extreme boredom events or showing off card tricks)
- Laser pointer that is not allowed in a carry-on
- Corkscrew (A good quality one with a foil cutter and cork-pry. (You never know when you will be in the Napa or Sonoma Valleys. Or, if in Portland, Oregon, you are not far from wineries in the Columbia Valley or the Willamette Valley wineries.)
- Identification/address label pasted inside the bag
- Copy of your passport picture page

Women warriors can add their weapons that include make up and many other necessities that I could never imagine. Most of the basics, however, including the Swiss Army toolkit, require no gender differences.

***

My carry-on bag of one of those small eighteen-inch, leather, computer roller bags that fits in any overhead compartment except for the upstairs level overheads of a 747 or the small Embraer-built commuter jets. It has top and outside zipper pockets to hold airline tickets and other items for quick retrieval. There is a side compartment, which is designed for a laptop, and even has a removable padded carrying bag if you want to protect the computer when removing it. The best thing about this style bag is that is doesn't look like a sissy man purse. Those are okay for women.

This type of bag can also be packed as an overnight bag with one change of clothes or it can be stuffed with camera equipment and vacation stuff for when you leisure travel.

It is a good idea to keep any prescriptions, especially the life saving ones, in your carry-on bag. Any, allergy, headache OTC products, including the Pepto, (Under 3 ½ ounce size) can be stored in this bag as well.

Below are suggestions for your business staples. Here is what I carry-on:

- Document holder for tickets, passport, receipts, traveler's checks and all your frequent flyer, stayer and renter cards.
- Pouch with noise cancelling headset and inflatable pillow and a metal pen. This pen is needed to fill out customs or immigration forms on the plane and it needs to be metal in case you need to stick it in a terrorist's temple or eye.
- Another pouch with three-way outlet, AC adapters and 12V car cell phone charger, GPS pickup for laptop GPS.
- Pens, marker and Sticky Note pad.
- Flash drive and external hard drive for laptop.
- Business cards and holder.
- Small Maglite™ flashlight.
- A few long cable ties are lifesavers if you break a luggage handle.

- A pack of extra batteries for your electronic stuff.
- USB gooseneck light for keyboard during long dark flights.
- Spare keys for your car and tradeshow booth-case padlocks if applicable.
- Another copy of your passport picture page.
- Laptop and related accessories.
- If traveling outside the U.S. be sure to include AC power adapters that will allow you to use your electrical travel items in the country you are visiting.
- The rest you will decide what to bring as needed.

Of course this is just my bag but if you follow a similar routine you will be pretty much covered in any emergency even if your checked bag is delayed. And if it sounds like over-kill; all that is mentioned is there because at one time, or times, it was needed.

One last suggestion: Go to your nearest electronics supply store and get some Velcro cable ties. This is the best way to keep the cords of all your chargers, headset and accessories neat and tidy. Get the kind that is slit at one end so you can slip the other end into it and permanently captivate it to the end of the cord you want to tie up.

Chapter 19

The Most Important Requirement

By now you must have realized that in order to be a successful road warrior you must possess qualities of intelligence, tenacity, adaptability, physical drive, a strong constitution and a good sense of humor. You need to be prepared to be away from home for up to ninety to one hundred and twenty days per year, or more. You need to know your business, your competition and your products inside and out. You cannot afford to waste your time or company's money and you need to keep records for purposes of follow up and follow through and doing what you said you would do. These are all things that you can control by yourself, and if done well your business life will run as smooth as you and Mister Murphy can guide it.

However, the one thing you cannot control is your spouse's, or significant other's, ability to accept your absences and your inability to be there all the time. Whether you travel a little or a lot, you need a person that is not riddled with insecurity, is self-sufficient and can fend for themselves when the dishwasher breaks, it snows, the kids are sick, or the car gets a flat tire. Most times this is as simple as calling "The Guy" to come and fix something. Opening a phonebook without complaining about the inconvenience is difficult for some.

I am one of those businessmen who is fortunate enough to have a wife that has handled the home situations during my absence for many years without the selfishness and whining that many other women would spew upon the one person who is trying to succeed in business for the gain of the family. I have heard of other women threatening the punishment routines of, "When you leave I'll go shopping and spend all your money," then finish the sentence with, "you bastard," or "you're cut-off."

Some spouses are clingy and unable to be mature or secure enough to handle the daily routine by themselves. That's not to say they don't get lonesome or afraid when they're alone. But large dogs or security systems should squelch the "afraid" problem and when you return you need to spend extra time appreciating them.

Without the support of your spouse or significant other you will fail. Flat out—you will not be able to do what is necessary to succeed. You will be made to feel guilty, you will be told, "You owe me," and "You're leaving me again?" and so you will always be looking to cut corners and not pursue the correct course to accomplish your ultimate goals.

It is a rare find to have someone who you can look to for support, understanding and trust so you can wear off your tail to the stump to earn the money and mileage points that treat the troops at home to some really nice vacations, among other things. I have been fortunate to have Mary as my partner in life who has the ability to deal with the every-day surprises and difficulties that life deals out. Without her support I would not have been able to capture the merit badge of success.

For this reason I dedicate this book to her. She is my love, my confidant, my supporter and my best friend.

***

I just heard the two bells signaling that we're on final approach and will be landing at Newark Liberty International in a few minutes. Finally. It has been a long flight and I didn't get a decent nap. Oh well, it's time to pack up the laptop and my headset, deflate my neck pillow, and hope my bag will be waiting for me in the baggage area today.

Ah, home again.

Breinigsville, PA USA
22 February 2011
256104BV00001B/4/P